CHICAGO BOUND

A Collection of Short Stories
and Things Remembered

Sandra Colbert

McIver Publishing
Freeport, IL

i

Copyright © 2015 by Sandra Colbert

ISBN: 978-0-9916227-6-4

Cover by digitalbookdesigns.com

Formatted by Lyle Ernst, lyleernst.com

Author's photo by Sarah Patnaude Photography

Printed in the United States of America

Published by McIver Publishing, Freeport, IL

The most common piece of advice given to writers is to get a good editor. In my case, I had a great editor.

My thanks to Ashley McDonald for her suggestions, corrections, her Oxford commas, and for giving confidence to a fledgling writer.

Many thanks to those who surround me, encourage me, and read the rough drafts.

And to Steve, for keeping the faith.

The works of poet, George Ella Lyon, became my inspiration for the poem "Origin."

*Dedicated to those
who came before me
and remain a part of me.*

INTRODUCTION

There is a time and a place in the history of Chicago that is fading away into the recesses of time. It was a place far removed from the realm of culture and sophistication being promoted in downtown Chicago at the turn of the last century. Some considered it the eighth wonder of the world and a tourist destination. And it was situated only a few miles south of the metropolis being created by the likes of Potter Palmer and Marshall Field.

The Chicago Stockyards was a place of exhaustion, of sweat and filth. This place, where thousands of animals were slaughtered on a weekly basis, was also the place where, for decades, masses of people toiled for meager wages and in wretched conditions. This time and place played a major role in shaping the city of Chicago.

It's hard to imagine what Chicago would look like had the financiers and politicians of the nineteenth century not brought the Stockyards to this burgeoning city – a city that had survived and was largely rebuilt after its devastating fire. It may have been the attitude that existed before or because of the fire – that nothing

v

was going to stop the growth, nothing was going to stop the prosperity of Chicago.

So, they brought in the railroads. Then they sectioned off acreage on what was then the southern edge of the city, and they built the pens and the packing plants. And the drovers brought in the animals.

The immigrant workers followed – first the Irish, then the Germans, followed by the Bohemians, the Polish, the Lithuanians, the Slovaks, and others from various regions of Europe, as well as the African Americans from the Southern States. As the stockyards grew, so did the immigrant population. Soon, segmented communities were created where the immigrants spoke the language of the country that they left behind.

The central institution of these communities was the churches, predominately Catholic Churches, built with the nickels and dimes of the immigrant stockyard worker.

Attached to each Catholic Church, there was the school. This is where the immigrant children were taught by nuns, usually until they were old enough to go to work. It was the parish church and school that, in so many ways, dominated and influenced the lives of their parishioners for decades.

These were the people who shaped the Bridgeport and the Back of the Yards neighborhoods, many of them living a life of extreme poverty in the crowded, tar-shingled, two and four flats of the area. It was these people who endured the brutal conditions that became the subject of Sinclair Lewis's book, *The Jungle.*

I, as well as thousands of others was born into this place. As the post-war baby boom erupted in Chicago and the surrounding suburbs, this community stayed very much the same. It was a community dominated by the Catholic Church, Democratic Party politics and an Eastern European culture.

At any given time you heard as much Lithuanian, Polish and Slovak as you did English. Single-family homes were the exception as most lived in flats, not apartments. Apartments were for the well-to-do in other parts of Chicago. There were taverns on nearly every block. The block I grew up on had three taverns at one point.

On warm, summer days the smell from the rendering plants lingered, not as strong, as in previous decades, I'm sure, but an odor I can still recall. There were cattle trucks rumbling down 47th street, bursting with the shrill sounds of bellowing animals. And yes, there was, and still is, a Bubbly Creek – a branch of the Chicago River that served as the communal sewer for the packers to dispose of the

vii

enormous wastes coming out of their plants. The putrefying, organic matter created gases or bubbles that gave it the innocuous name.

It was as an adult that I realized my childhood memories were unique. We were caught in between two worlds: the old world of customs, food and languages of other countries and the new world of television, TV dinners and rock-and-roll. There was the junk collector on his wooden wagon drawn by a horse clomping down the alley. He was as much a part of the neighborhood as the teenage boys standing on the corner with their slicked back hair and James Dean attitudes.

I'm sure the thousands of immigrants that came to this country and endured these things looked to the future, not solely for themselves, but for their children and the children of their children. Their endurance was a mark of the love they had for their children and the country and families they had left behind.

Ironically, a sign of success was moving out of the area, perhaps to Marquette Park or even further to the suburbs. So we left, the children and the children of the children, many determined to not look back, embarrassed by their roots.

Writing these short works of fiction was a reflective look back at that time and place which is now long gone. Not always flattering, the stories are a response to the environs of my youth and also an appreciation of those who endured so much for so little.

The Stone Gate, the entrance to the Union Stock yards, built by Daniel Burnham and John Root stands today as a Chicago landmark. And then there is us - the generations of college students, of soldiers, of businessmen and women, of police officers, of dedicated parents - the legacy of those who bravely left all they knew for the unknown that lay ahead of them.

S. Colbert

TABLE OF CONTENTS

Origin

I am from sweat I am from
tears
I am from the salt of the ocean
waves
I am from fear and survival
Graveyard dirt and mossy
headstones
I am from broken language
Gothic spires
Black clad nuns and sermons
on fire
I am from hunger and anger
I am from love, the word left
unspoken

THE DEADLINE

Another summer and, as always,
my thoughts go back to '48.

I covered the Yards for the dailies a lot
of years. It was my beat, for better, for
worse. I figured my editor hated me.

Chicago is my home. I was born here.
I've been all over this city. I know it.

I know where the swells live on the
north side. I can find the smack dealers in
Little Tokyo. You want the name of the
best strippers in town, just ask. And in case
you're interested, I can show you where the
Cardinal lives. Like I said, I know this burg.

But the Back of the Yards, well, it's
like no other place in the city. Where else
can you wait for a streetcar while a truck
goes by hauling squealing animals? And the
smell - it's a stench that you don't forget.

I was the outsider, the Irish guy. All
around me, they spoke mostly Polish,
Lithuanian and who knows what all? Most
of the time, they spoke enough English so
that I was able to understand them.

They were a tough breed. Not that
different from my people. They lived hard
lives. During the long days at the
Stockyards, they slaughtered pigs and

cows. At night, on weekends, they drank. I know that kind of drink. It's a drink to forget. It's a mean drink.

On paydays, the women waited outside of the entrances of the yards, sometimes with a kid or two in tow, to get their hands on the paychecks before the money was squandered away on bad booze. There were kids to feed.

The taverns were on just about every block. One block had three of them. Not that long ago they had Whiskey Row. An entire block of shabby bars where you could drink yourself blind and no one cared. They would just push you out the door at the end of the night and leave you lying there. You figure out how to get home.

The city finally cleaned things up. There's a furniture store there now and other legitimate, polished businesses. But that didn't stop these people from finding a joint that'll give them a cheap shot and beer. Even during Prohibition, they just made their own rot gut in a bathtub. Yeah, like I said, this was my beat.

Not a lot to cover for a Chitown reporter. Bar fights happened all the time. So I covered the politicians, the big shots. Not too much of anything else in the Back of the Yards, aside from the occasional fire or robbery. I once saw a small kid, a five year old boy, get hit by a car. He was killed. The mother didn't seem to be too broke up about it. Heck, she had seven more at her squalid little apartment. She was a widow. Her husband was killed when he got caught between two railroad cars at the coal yard. Now there's a story that I'm glad I missed.

One night it was different.

It was a steamy, summer night - humid and rank. I went to Frank's, one of the better watering holes. He kept his place clean and didn't put up with much. Things had been quiet for too long and I was itching for a story. So was my editor. I figured I'd hang out with the locals. A few boilermakers, and who knew? Maybe I could come up with a story. I knew a lot of these guys and for the most part, I didn't mind their company.

I'm sitting next to Bruno, a beast of a man. He'd been at the Yards for a lot of years, and slaughtered a lot of cows. He had the arms to prove it. Big and mean was Bruno.

Strangely enough, Bruno liked me. Maybe it was my red hair and slight build, but he always made a point of sitting by me at the bar and making small talk.

So in comes Joey. Joey stayed clear of the Yards and worked as a mechanic at a small garage down the street. He knew his cars. Joey was one hell of a good looking guy and a real wolf. Dark hair, dark eyes, like the movie star, John Garfield. The babes loved Joey and Joey loved the babes.

And Joey loved to kiss and tell.

This particular night, Joey was in a bragging mood, especially after a shot and beer.

He had a new babe. And he scored big time. A real beauty, natural blond, blue eyes and what a figure. Real good in the sack, Joey says, grinning. She could be a show girl at one of those fancy North Side Clubs. He should have stopped there and then.

But no, he tells me she works at a bakery on 47th Street.

I could feel the air change. And then he tells me, she's married to some Polish lug who works at the Stockyards.

Poor Joey never knew what hit him. I didn't know Bruno could move so fast.

"You screw my vife! You son a bitch! You screw my vife!" was all I heard as Bruno picked up Joey and flung him across the room. He kept screaming as he pummeled Joey's head into the floor.

There were four of us on Bruno, but he kept shaking us off. He didn't let up until Frank came up to him with the sawed off shotgun that he kept behind the bar for just such an occasion.

"Get out of my bar" Frank said very calmly as he stuck the gun in Bruno's mug.   "If I ever see you near this place again I will blow your stupid Polack brains out. Now get out."

"He fuck my vife! The bastard, he fuck my vife." Bruno yelled breathlessly. "Too god damn bad." Frank replied. "Just get the hell out of here."

He shook us off and headed for the door, but not before spitting at the bloody mess that was now Joey.

"Call an ambulance, then the cops." Frank ordered.

There were differing stories when it came to what happened to Bruno's wife. Some people said she was warned and took off before Bruno got home. Some of the others said they heard some screaming and saw Bruno walking down the alley carrying a bundle heading towards the cesspool that everyone called Bubbly Creek.

All I know is nobody in the neighborhood ever saw her again. Bruno told people, including the cops, that the tramp he married moved to the north side where she had some relatives. The cops said her clothes and her purse were still in the flat.

No one told the cops anything. No one was going to cross Bruno. Joey was in no condition to press charges. The cops wrote it off as another barroom brawl.

So Bruno ended up moving into a basement flat in Bridgeport. He didn't miss a day's work.

Joey, well Joey missed a lot work. Actually, he could never really work again.

When he finally got out of the hospital his face was so messed up you could hardly recognize the poor slug. The gals wouldn't be chasing him anymore. He walked with a limp now and he drooled. That wasn't even the worst of it. His brain took a real hit. Half the time he couldn't even count to ten much less fix a carburetor. His mother took care of him like he was a kid again. Frank gave him a job wiping tables and sweeping up at the end of the night. Poor Joey, he never knew what hit him.

My editor told me to forget it. It was just another fight in just another filthy bar by the Yards. Not worth a byline. But I snooped around anyway. I wanted to find the girl or at least, find out the truth about what happened to the girl.

But nobody was talking. You could see the fear in their eyes when I mentioned Bruno and what happened at Frank's. I got as much information as the cops did, which amounted to nothing.

The girl deserved better. She shouldn't be rotting at the bottom of Bubbly Creek with the sludge from the stockyards.

But it bothered me. It bothered me a lot. It bothered me to see feeble minded Joey.

And it ate me up inside that Bruno got away with what he did.

So I quit the newspaper business. Now I sell carpets on the North Side. But on hot muggy Chicago nights, all these years later, I can still smell the Yards. And I can still see Joey's messed up face. And I still think about the girl. I like to think that maybe someday she'll come into my store with her husband and a baby and buy a carpet from me. But I know deep down, that will never happen.

ABOUT A LOVE

This is a story that should be told. It happened when I was a boy in the old neighborhood – back in 1953.

There was a couple - Andrew and Polly, who ran a little grocery store on the corner, across from the priests' rectory. They were very well liked. They moved from a small town in southern Indiana in the late 30's and opened their little store in our neighborhood. Every July without fail, they would close the store for 3 weeks and go back to their hometown for a visit.

Polly ran the store during the day while Andrew went to work as a salesman at the shoe store a few blocks away. They weren't fluent in Polish or Lithuanian, which so many in the area spoke, but they made a point of learning enough to make their customers happy.

Polly loved children, so it was especially sad that she didn't have any. She was gentle and sweet to all of the children in the neighborhood, usually doling out little penny candies to them when they came into the store or even when she came across them playing out in the street. Polly always carried little hard candy treats with her.

It was the same with Andrew at the shoe store. He was everyone's favorite salesman. The children liked him for his humor. He could be so silly with them, tickling the bottom of their feet while he measured them for their new shoes or doing a Porky Pig imitation.

The ladies liked him for his patience as they tried on so many pairs of shoes. He always seemed to know what looked best on them.

Andrew and Polly had each other. Andrew could be described as round. He was short, with a round head that held his big horned rim glasses. Polly could be described as pudgy with short, graying brown hair that complemented her gentle brown eyes. You would often see them hand in hand, strolling through our little park on warm spring evenings.

The couple loved their parish church and were active in it, volunteering for whatever events that were coming up. You would see them every Sunday and holy day sitting in the same pew.

One day Andrew was shopping in the men's department of the Goldblatt's Store in our neighborhood. After he made his purchase he walked over to the stairs leading down to the main floor. Suddenly he clutched his chest in pain. Seconds later he collapsed and fell down the stairs. He was dead before he hit the landing.

As he fell down the stairs his shirt got caught on something and was torn open. When the other customers ran to his aid, it was obvious to them that Andrew was not a man. When the ambulance came and he was rushed to the hospital, it was declared that he was not only dead but also, was not a man.

But even before Andrew reached the hospital, the news spread through the telephone lines like wildfire. If you didn't have a phone someone was knocking on your door to relate to you the most shocking news since Pearl Harbor, in their estimation.

Before the Police or someone from the hospital had the opportunity to tell Polly, one of the parish priests, the pastor no less, walked into the small grocery store. As usual Polly greeted him with her warm smile. When he put the CLOSED sign on the door her smile faded.

He told her that Andrew was dead, a heart attack. Before she had time to absorb the news, he told her to pray for their souls. He told her how they not only lived in Mortal sin, but that their lives together was of the most deviate, the most shameful and the most disgusting that he had ever seen. God was surely punishing her for the deceitful life that they led. And then he walked out slamming the door behind him.

Polly collapsed and wept until she could weep no longer. That was where the policeman found her. He helped her to her feet, brought her to her kitchen and made sure the store was locked up and consoled her as best he could. No one from the neighborhood came to see her.

They were too busy being stunned. As they spoke to each other they ran the children out of the room. This was not for young ears. Many of them felt deceived, and foolish, as if someone played a terrible joke on them. So they lashed out, saying that they suspected something was not right - that they never really liked the two of them very much to begin with. They said a lot of things that were not true.

Polly was very much alone when she appeared in front of the undertaker. He was distinctly uncomfortable for someone who had seen so much in his long career. When he said that he would provide the dress and would have someone do her hair and makeup he was suddenly confronted with a very different Polly. She had brought with her a shopping bag. When she removed Andrew's suit from it, he was horrified. A long and loud argument ensued.

But they worked out a solution. Andrew, whose birth name was Anna, would be buried in a suit, but it would be a closed casket, something that was reserved for the very maimed and mutilated.

The next day was the wake. Wakes, regardless of who you were, were usually attended by most of the people in the neighborhood. It was a close-knit community and not attending a wake for someone, especially a shopkeeper, was considered a huge snub. Polly sat alone. A few relatives from Indiana showed up, said a few prayers, shed a few tears, but did not stay long.

My buddy Chester, and I decided to go. Driven by all the adult secret conversations, curiosity got the better of us. Besides, I really liked Polly and Andrew and I felt bad that he died. I couldn't understand a lot of what was being said in the whispering around me.

We didn't tell anyone and headed for the funeral home. We picked up a few more of our friends on the way. This little caravan of scruffy boys quietly signed the book that had the name "Anna" on it and went into the dimly lit parlor.

We were confused not only by the name in the book and on the sign by the door, but by the closed coffin. We shrugged our shoulders a lot as we walked over to the casket to pray. But it was the shock of seeing Polly sitting all alone in that funeral parlor that affected me the most. No one else was there. It's an image I never forgot.

I'll also never forget Polly's expression when she saw us. Behind her tears there was a look of such relief and affection, it choked me up. She gave us all hugs as we told her, in our awkward way, how bad we felt. We could tell she didn't want us to leave so we stayed a while. We talked about baseball cards and the new Chevy that someone's dad had bought. We were loud and irreverent. She seemed so interested, so pleased.

A few people showed up for the funeral. The priest refused to say a mass. He would only preside over a short funeral service that included a few prayers and a lot of incense. The ones who showed up did so mostly out of curiosity. They patted her on the back, mumbled a few awkward words and fled. No one went to the cemetery. I was there because I was the altar boy who assisted the priest. Polly smiled when she saw me. I saw her tears and her pain. I was holding back my own tears.

Within a couple of weeks, she closed her shop and moved away. I didn't know where. She didn't speak to anyone after the funeral unless she had to. She didn't tell anyone where she was going. One day she was just gone. I went on with my life as a kid.

Fifteen years later, I had my teaching degree and my first job was at a grammar school in a south Chicago suburb. As I was walking down the hallway getting acclimated to my new surroundings, I spotted the cleaning lady coming in my direction carrying her supplies. I smiled to her as she passed me. Then I froze in my steps. It was Polly. I called to her. There was absolute joy on her face when she realized who I was, then absolute fear. I understood the fear. Quietly, and in an almost coded way, I let her know that I would never share our story from the past with anyone in our present.

She told me about the intervening years. She moved to a small apartment in this particular suburb because she wanted to be close to the cemetery where Andrew was buried. Up to that point, she had never learned to drive but living in a suburb, she was suddenly forced to learn. It turned out that she loved to drive and loved the freedom that it gave her. The job at the school was a godsend, she said. She was surrounded by small children and few adults. Her life was a solitary one. She never went to church again, but volunteered at every charity that she could. Her life was good and it pleased me to hear that.

Polly tended to Andrew's grave often. If anyone asked if she had been married, she spoke of her late husband with such affection that it saddened the person that she was speaking to.

I've just come from Polly's funeral. We laid her to rest next to Andrew. It says Andrew on the headstone. She had total control when it came to the name on the headstone. It was a large funeral with adults who remembered her from their grammar school years and came to love her as I did. No one from the old neighborhood was there, except my old buddy Chester.

We kept her secret, honored her request. But in my mind it's a story that should be told.

Love being what it is.

A CONFESSION

July, 1972

The old man looked down at his trembling hands. They were once so strong and sure, he thought. Now they shake. *I'm not a scared old man*, he reassured himself. *I've been here too long.* He went back to staring out the window. The same second floor window he had looked out of during the many decades he had lived in this house. The same bedroom he had slept in for so many years.

Too much has changed, he thought. The houses he saw were the same houses, but different people came and went. He could still see the faces of the ones from years ago and remember their names, even the towns and villages that they came from. They were gone; most were dead or had moved away, except for him. Their children didn't want to be part of this neighborhood. At one time he had been an important man in this neighborhood - a leader, one of the founders of the large Catholic Church a block away, a man who helped fellow immigrants, a man that many came to for advice. Now he was just the funny old man who had turned one hundred.

He heard a noise and saw his teenage grandson standing in the doorway. The young man lived with his parents and brother in the downstairs flat. They looked after him and he didn't charge them rent, although he would be the first to admit that he didn't need anyone to care for him. He had no problems getting around, and he always able to do his own cooking and cleaning. But he was glad that they were there.

"Hi Gramps" said the lanky young man. "How ya doing today. Need anything?"

"No, No" he responded. "I'm alright. Did you eat?"

"Ma's making dinner now." He paused. "Ya ready for the party tomorrow? How's it feel? Ya know, being a hundred?"

The old man stared silently at the young man.

"Sit" he ordered. "Sit."

The boy retrieved a chair and sat.

"A hundred. A hundred." He shook his head. "I no can believe it. I tell you about a hundred. How old you now?"

"I'll be eighteen next month."

"Good. I tell you. Only you. You a man now, so I tell you." The young man suddenly felt uncomfortable.

"I come to this country from Lithuania. There the rotten Russians, they come to my village, take me away, and put me in their army. They make me fight the Japs. I learn how to kill with these hands, with these strong hands. I not get killed. So when the war over, I come here, away from the Russians."

"Never see my village, my people again." He paused to collect his thoughts.

"I do what I have to do. I learn English. I learn my numbers. I learn to read. I can write little. I not let no one treat me like I stupid because I no speak English. I learn enough. I work in stockyards. Worse job. Blood and stink everywhere."

He let out a long sigh. "Barbara, my first wife. She so pretty. See her picture."

"Yeah" the boy responded as he looked over at the picture on the dresser. The picture had been there as long as he could remember. The sepia tone wedding picture was of a young girl in her wedding gown, unsmiling, standing next to a handsome, mustached, also unsmiling, young man.

"She was a whore." the old man said calmly.

"What?" was all the boy could say, hoping he had misunderstood the old man.

"She was a whore on the street. I see her on the street with the other girls. I hear her talk. She speak from my country. You know?"

"She was Lithuanian, like you, you mean?"

"Yes, I talk to her. She from my village. She was little girl when I left. The man who sells her and the others, what you call them, I not know."

"Like... a pimp, you, you mean?" The young man stammered.

"Yeah, what you call bastard like that. He watch me. Then say I can't look. I must buy. I go around block. He not see me come from behind. I break his neck like a chicken. Then I throw him in alley with other garbage." The old man began to breathe heavily. His eyes reflected the rage that never left him.

The young man froze. His stomach clenched as he tried to absorb what he was hearing.

"I grab Barbara and we run. We go on streetcar. I take her to this house. We get married." He looked out of the window again. "You do what you have to do! You hear me."

"Yeah, yeah, Gramps," he paused. "You killed this guy. You killed him"

"She so pretty, so good." He was somewhere else again. "They say she die of cancer. Not cancer. She die of filthy disease that men give her when she was a whore. But she not ever a whore. They made her do these things. And she die young and with no children."

The young man looked at the picture, unable to utter a sound.

The old man looked lost in thought.

His grandson was not sure if he would continue.

"I love her."

There was only the sound of their breathing breaking the silence.

"In ten years, I meet your grandmother. We get married. She think I rich because I own this building." He began to laugh. "I show her. I not have a pot to piss in. She not get money from me. Her kids hate me. I don't care. I don't care."

"But her kids have kids," he continued. "And they like me. Yes. You like me. Yes?" He paused when he saw this grandson nodding.

"Yeah, Gramps, I like you a lot."

He put his shaking hands on the young man's shoulders.

"You always a good boy. But I learn. You listen to old man. You do what you have to do. You know what this means?"

"Yeah, Yeah, Gramps. I guess so."

"You a man now. Not a boy no more. This is being a man," the old man said looking into the eyes of the young man.

"You do what you have to do." He repeated.

"Yes, Gramps. Okay," said the grandson, not sure how to respond.

"You go downstairs now. Go eat. Okay?"

"Okay, okay." The young man softly responded. He couldn't stop the shiver that came up through his stomach. "I'll... I'll see you tomorrow"

"No tomorrow. You no come.

It's Saturday. You sleep. Tell your father to come in morning."

"Yeah, okay Gramps." he said. As he left the room he looked down at his trembling hands.

After the young man left, the old man let out a long sigh. He looked out the window. It had gotten too dark to see anything. He stood up slowly, went to the dresser and removed a frayed velvet case. From it he removed a straight edge razor. He caressed the ivory handle which was as beautiful as it was sixty years earlier when he bought it from a Jewish peddler on Maxwell Street.

He took the razor as well as the wedding picture from the dresser and carried them to the bathroom.

From the closet he took his suit and his best shirt and tie. He laid them on the sofa.

Returning to the bathroom, while never taking his eyes off the picture of him and Barbara, the old man removed his clothes and lay down in the tub.

Then the old man did what he had to do.

ABRAHAM

They called him The Jew, as if that was his name, my grandmother and her lady friends. Our neighborhood in the 1950's was predominately Lithuanian and Polish and very Catholic, so a little Jewish man with the limp stood out. But oh, how they looked forward to his visits. He came every few weeks, always on a Saturday, carrying his large bulky suitcase. A suitcase of wares which included an assortment of scarves, hairnets, doilies, brushes and all other bright and lacy things, which he carefully laid out on the dining room table for Grandma and her friends to admire.

Soon he had them twittering and opening their purses. He spoke just enough Lithuanian and Polish to close a sale and to flatter the ladies. But he always ignored me.

I tried to ingratiate myself by doing my share of ohhing and ahhing, but he acted like I wasn't there. This did not go well for my 10-year-old ego. I was used to adults fawning over me. They liked my blond hair, my outgoing ways, my almost adult bantering and the fact that I made an effort to speak their language. Not

25

very well, but I tried. But this man, well, he just never saw any of my obvious charms. So I was usually shooed out of the house when he showed up, much to my annoyance, I might add.

So on one of these Saturdays, for no other reason than I was bored, I decided to follow him. He went to a few other houses on my block. I waited patiently. Then he went on to the next block. He stopped to wipe his forehead, and then took out a set of keys, and I knew he was going home. He headed toward a three flat and started down the few stairs to the basement apartment when he looked up and saw me. Strangely enough it didn't bother me that I was caught following him. I smiled my most beguiling smile. He didn't smile back.

"Are you Mrs. Leshinski's grand-daughter?"

"Yeah."

"What do you want?" He wasn't warming up to me.

I had to think fast. I really didn't know what I wanted, but I couldn't tell him that.

"Um, I want to buy something."

"You want to buy something?"

He frowned. "So, you follow me to my house."

"It's a surprise. I suddenly had a great idea. "It's for my mother. Her birthday is next Friday, and I want to get her something."

"So, what is it you want? I don't have all day."

"The brush. The pretty one with the jewels on the back."

To my shock, he began to laugh, and laugh very hard.

"What's so funny?" I didn't appreciate being laughed at.

"Jewels. Yes, I sell brushes encrusted with precious jewels. Yes, rubies, sapphires, only the best for the ladies in this neighborhood." He wiped his eyes.

"You know what I mean. That pretty one that you showed my grandmother." Now I was the one who was irritated.

"So Miss Fancypants, you got some money for this big purchase?"

"I don't know. How much is it?"

"For this extraordinary brush, one dollar."

Hmm, I had eleven cents in my piggybank at home.

"I don't have it with me, but I could get it."

"Well, when you have it, come back and I'll sell you the brush." "Fine," I said. "I'll be back on Friday morning."

"Yeah, yeah," he said as he turned his back on me and went into his flat.

I know I was frowning as I walked back to my house. I took an alternate route through the alley. I had to start then and there if I was going to get the money for this brush. It was a matter of principle now. I would show him that I was serious and not some silly neighborhood kid. And I knew my mother really would like that brush for her birthday.

So, first things first- soda pop bottles. I kept my eyes open for them. At two cents for every returned bottle I could accumulate something. Then there were my two older brothers. The oldest, Tommy, worked at a gas station. I could probably get some of the money from him. And Richie delivered newspapers. He would probably pitch in. And if I ran errands for my grandmother, she was good for a couple of nickels. I was very pleased with myself as I strolled through the alley looking for pop bottles.

By Friday, I had the money. It was in nickels, dimes and one quarter, but I had it. I put the coins in my little, plastic purse and sauntered down my block looking every bit the sophisticated shopper.

When he opened the door, he actually looked shocked to see me. "I'm here to buy the brush."

"So I see. Come in. Come in. Such an important customer, she even has a purse." He had a slight smile on his face. I was hoping he wouldn't start laughing at me again.

I walked directly into the kitchen of his small flat. There was a cup of coffee on the table sitting next to an open book. If you looked out of the window, you could see the feet of the people walking by. That fact, for some strange reason, fascinated me.

"You like my little dwelling?" He asked.

"Yes, It's, um, charming." Obviously a comment that I heard on television.

"Well, you just wait here. I'll go find your brush." He walked into what must have been the living room.

As I was putting the money on the table, I noticed a picture on the table. It was in a plain silver frame - a picture of a younger version of this man, standing behind a seated woman, with dark, upswept hair and dark eyes. She was lovely. To her left stood a young girl about my age, also with dark hair, worn long and wavy. On the woman's right was a young boy, probably about four or five, with the same dark hair and dark eyes. They all looked content - solid and content. It was a beautiful photograph of a beautiful family.

"Oye, I almost could not..," his voice trailed off when he saw the picture in my hand. He went silent.

"You have kids?" I said looking around for evidence of such.

"Kids? Do I have kids?" He put the brush down and took the picture from my hands. He stared vacantly at the photo. I remained silent.

"Children. Do I have children?" He said so softly that I could hardly hear him. "Once, I did."

I was confused. "Once?"

"Before they came, the Nazis." His voice went flat. "Before they came and took us. All of us. Mama and her children in one direction and me in another. They put them on a train and took them to a prison and killed them and burned their beautiful bodies. So, do I have children? I have memories of children and a wife, my family."

He took his eyes off the picture and looked at me. I had never seen, or have seen since, the look of total anguish, of such pain.

But I was just a child. I was horrified. The words were sinking in and I couldn't comprehend them. I remember covering my face, not breathing, and then simply running out of his flat and down the street.

I ran up the stairs to our flat and burst through the kitchen door. Thankfully, my mother was there getting ready to bake cookies.

"What in God's name?" she said when she saw me. I was breathing hard and trying not to cry.

"You know who the Jew is Mom?"

"Yeah, of course, what's going on? What happened?" She looked scared.

"Did you know? Did you know about his kids, his children and his wife?"

"Wait. Just calm down and tell me what's going on."

So I sputtered out the details, in fits and starts.

"Oh Kristine, what am I going to do with you?" she said when I finished. "Can't you just mind your own business? You should have never bothered that poor man. You just leave him alone and don't go there again."

"OK." It was all that I was able to say.

She brought me a glass of water and sat down next to me.

31

"Horrible things happened in the war, just horrible. Did you see the numbers on his left arm?" she asked.

"No."

"Well, grandma and I and others on the block have seen them. That was his number when he was in the prison camp. So we all had a good idea of what happened to him, but we never asked. We knew it was horrible, and it would do no good to bring it up. And so we buy from him, and we're nice to him. That's all we can do. It's in the past." She stood up and resumed her work on the cookies.

"Mom?"

"What?"

"Do you know his name?" She looked out the window with a puzzled expression and then back at me.

"No, no I don't."

As I stood in front of his building that following morning, I knew I was committing a sin by disobeying my mother. But I planned on going to confession that afternoon and would confess this sin and take whatever penance the priest dealt out. Some things just had to be done. I was sure God would understand.

When he answered the door, he did not look at all surprised to see me. "Well, you come back. You left your brush here, you know."

"Yes, I know. I should not have run away. I'm sorry about that." He looked down at me and nodded his head.

"Come in," he said gently. "I'm sorry. I forget sometimes. You are too young. You should be left alone to be a child. So it's me who should be sorry."

"It's okay. I brought you some cookies. I hope you like them. My mother makes real good cookies. Everyone says so." Somewhere in the back of my mind I knew that when someone in your family dies, people bring food. It just seemed to me that I had to bring him food, even though what happened to him had happened a long time ago.

"Thank you. I am sure they are very good." I saw a small smile on his worn face. "Here is your brush."

"Thank you. Can I ask you something?"

"So ask." He nodded.

I looked at the picture again. I hadn't noticed it before, but there was a small vase in front of it with four plastic lily of the valley flowers in it.

"What are their names?"

He seemed surprised at the question. Then he slowly, reverentially picked up the picture and looked at it for what seemed like a long time. I was afraid he wouldn't answer me.

The pretty lady-she is Estelle, my wife. Such beautiful hair. Such dark eyes. He paused and sighed. "The little girl Sara, is about your age in this picture-smart, pretty like her mother. Don't you think?"

"Yes, she is very pretty" I replied. And I meant it.

"And the little boy. That is David. Always running and getting into mischief. But laughing, always laughing. You cannot stay mad at him."

"You have a nice family."

"Had. Little one. I had a nice family." We were both silent for a while.

"I was wondering," I said softly, "would it be alright with you, I know you're not a Catholic, but would it be okay, if when I go to mass tomorrow, that I say a rosary for Estelle and Sara and David."

I saw the mist in his eyes.

"That would be good. Yes, that would be a nice thing to do. I do not pray much anymore. So your prayer, your rosary, that would be good." He said. "Thank you."

He gave me the picture to hold. I knew I wouldn't forget their faces. They looked so untouched and pure.

"Can I ask you something else?"

"Of course."

"What is your name?"

He smiled a real smile for the first time.

"My name is Abraham Blumenthal. You may call me Abraham."

"Like the president."

"Yes, like the president. And little one, what is your name?"

"Kristine, with a K." I smiled back.

"Kristine, with a K. So modern. A very nice name. Mrs. Leshinski has a very nice granddaughter."

"Thank you." I put the picture back on the table and put the little vase in front of it. "I better go."

"Yes, and I have my ladies to visit. I'm sure they have many purchases to make. " He said. "Don't forget the brush. I hope your mother likes it."

"She will. I know she will."

"Good bye, Kristine." He smiled.

"Good bye, Abraham." I smiled back and left after glancing one more time at the picture on the table.

I saw Abraham several times after that. He always greeted me with, "Hello, Kristine," and I always responded with "Hello, Abraham." This always raised the eyebrows of anyone who heard this. I never let my grandmother or my mother call him anything but Abraham. I never told them how I found out his name.

On a late September day, my grandmother came over to our flat. "Your friend, Abraham," she said to me.

"Yeah, what about him?"

"He won't be coming around anymore."

"What! What are you talking about, Grandma?" I felt my chest tense up.

"He moved away. Sophie just told me. She talked to Joe, his landlord. He said he packed up and moved away, just yesterday."

"No, no he didn't." I was shocked. It seemed like something that I should have known. He was my friend. He would have told me. He couldn't just be gone. I ran out the flat before my grandmother or mother could stop me. I ran as fast as I could to his building.

The door to the flat was open, and Joe was inside sweeping.

I stood there and stared at the bare flat, at the kitchen table with no picture. Joe saw me. He knew who I was.

"He's gone?" I said.

"Yeah, he left yesterday, He went to live with his brother on the north side. Didn't give me much notice. I'm sorry to see him go. A good tenant, paid his rent on time. No problems. Quiet."

I didn't know what to say. But I wanted to cry. It didn't make sense, and Joe wouldn't have understood, but I wanted to cry. He left without saying good bye.

"He said you might be around. He told me to give you this if you showed up."

With that said, he handed me the little vase with the plastic lily of the valley flowers. I took it and walked toward my church. I needed to be alone. Nobody would understand. I didn't understand.

I still have the little vase. It's a little chipped and a little worn. It's been everywhere with me, and every spring, I fill it with live lily of the valley flowers.

And when I do, I say a prayer, make a wish, and entreat a higher power that somehow, some way, Abraham is with his family again.

EASTER

This is what we remember...

I remember practicing in the church and getting excited over what I was going to get to carry (Bells, clapper or incense) while listening to the choir practice. I remember Holy Saturday when the people would bring the food to be blessed and I remember kneeling at the altar for hours with another altar boy and with the men from the Knights of Columbus. The altar railing was loaded with so many breads and different foods. I remember getting hungry.

I remember taking the baskets with Grandma's homemade bread and our colored eggs, the eggs that we decorated the night before, to the Church to be blessed.

I remember not being sleepy even though it was the middle of the night. It was exciting being up at that time. I remember grandma and mom fussing over my hair and making sure my white blouse, blue skirt and veil was perfect. We were Sodality girls and we had verses to sing during the procession.

I remember walking up the main steps of the church, going in and hearing the choir. All the bells were ringing. I remember walking with the other altar boys in front of the priests. It was a long procession, going around the huge church three times.

I remember Uncle Ed, who went to church twice a year, trying to make me laugh every time I walked by him.

I remember getting chills when the choir sang the Handel's Messiah Chorus. It was magnificent. I remember feeling so proud of the beautiful church filled with so many lilies and smell of incense and the first light of dawn coming through the stained glass windows.

I remember everything in different shades of pastel and gold. The vestments of the priests, the flowers, the women in their Easter outfits standing in front of the church after the mass, smiling and chatting with each other, the men in suits and wearing fedoras were laughing.

I remember trying to stay clean after we got home and I changed into my Easter dress. Pictures were going to be taken. Company was coming. Grandma gave us cups of coffee and bacon buns to keep us going until all of the relatives showed up.

I don't remember much after the procession and the mass. I remember being at home where the ladies were cooking. We would have polish sausage, ham, our decorated hard boiled eggs, grandma's homemade bread and more. After we ate, the ladies cleaned the kitchen and the men sat around the table drinking. Later that afternoon some were asleep on the couch. I went outside to play.

This is what we were meant to remember.

MY SANTA

1955

We tend to revere memories of Christmases past, but for some, it's a difficult search for a single gold nugget in the hardscrabble earth.

One of my earliest memories of Christmases past involved, like many a young girl, my desire for a doll. All my friends and cousins had dolls and I didn't have one. But it was more than that. It was a longing I could not explain. The air surrounding my family was so dark. And I was trying so hard to be good, but that wasn't enough. In my child's mind, I just knew that a doll would make things better.

There are periods in one's life when times are not good and it's difficult for a child to understand, since it is fallout from the adult world. But I remember once asking my grandmother if Mommy was still sick, and all she said, so very softly, was "yes". I asked her if we were poor, and all she said, once again, softly but firmly, was "yes".

I recall moving into my grandparents' bungalow with my two older brothers and my father. My mother was not with us. She was sick and in the hospital. I had memories of my mother being funny and affectionate. But they were vague memories that I would try to retrieve, hoping to recapture them, especially at night when the house was dark and filled with strange noises. During those times I just wanted my Mommy.

So much was kept from me. I think the family thought I was simply too young to understand. Yes, seven is young, but so much gets absorbed. And so much is left in a cloud of confusion. I learned the word "cancer" from hearing my grandmother praying at the kitchen table when she thought she was alone. She was beseeching God to remove the cancer from her daughter.

My mother came home on several occasions. A visitor, home long enough for her family to think she was getting better. But then something would happen, usually in the middle of the night and she would disappear again - an unmade bed left in her wake.

The most recent time that she came home it was almost Thanksgiving, grey and stark. I was brought to her room to see her. But it was not the Mother that I knew. Instead, a gaunt woman, with dark eyes, her skin stretched over bone, a huge white bandage wrapped around her head, sat there. Her thin arms were outstretched, waiting for me. I couldn't move, even with my grandmother and my brothers behind me telling me to go give Mommy a kiss. Instead, I tried to run out of the room. Terrified of what, I did not know.

Finally, she told them to let me go. So I ran. I ran to my bed and crawled underneath it. I hid there for hours. I was sleeping when my grandfather pulled me out. He didn't scold me. I think he understood. I didn't.

And now she was in the hospital again. My father was barely making enough for us to get by before the doctor bills came in, so we were forced to move in with my Grandparents. When Daddy wasn't working at the factory down the street, he was visiting my mother or sitting in the little bar on the corner sipping a beer with his few friends. We hardly saw him and when we did, it seemed to me that he still wasn't there.

On rare evenings, he would take out the photo albums and smile. Those evenings were special. He would put me on his lap and point out a picture, then tell me where it was taken and who was in it. It was the wedding pictures that I enjoyed the most – my mother so beautiful, my father so handsome. Everyone smiling. I wished that there was a magic that could transport me into those pictures, where I could laugh and dance with all of those happy people

Gramma was left to raise us. For Gramma, life was nothing but a series of obstacles and tragedies to be overcome. She was a dour woman, not quick to smile or laugh. But she was a survivor, proud and tough. Gramma came to America in steerage from Eastern Europe, leaving everything and everyone that she knew behind. She worked at the stockyards, dealt with the Depression, and sent two sons to war. Only one came back.

Now her only daughter was sick, so very sick.

Gramma had no time for the childish wishes of toys, dolls or the nonsense of Santa Claus.

Gramps, well, Gramps was a quiet, gentle man who stayed in the background. He held me when I needed to be held and played with me when I needed to be played with. I loved him unconditionally. Unlike Gramma, he was quick to laugh and loved to tell me stories that he heard as a child in Lithuania.

My brothers were much older than me.
Teddy was fifteen, and Paul was twelve.
At times they referred to me as an
"accident". I never understood what they
meant. But I went to them when I needed
help with my request for a doll from Santa
Claus. They told me that there was no
such thing as Santa Claus. But I wrote a
letter anyway. Brothers could be wrong.
Gramps said he would take it to the
mailbox for me.

Christmas Eve came, and off we all
went to Midnight mass, which in itself is
now a marvelous memory of carols sung
by a brilliant choir in a huge gothic style
church decorated so beautifully. I just
knew that Mary, Joseph and baby Jesus
were watching only us and were glad to
be in our church.

On Christmas morning, in spite of the
late night, we woke early. Gramma
prepared a big breakfast. Uncles, Aunts,
and cousins were expected later in the day
for dinner. The adults had plans to go to
the hospital to visit my mother. I drew
some pictures for them to take to her. I
missed her. But I didn't know how to tell
her.

No matter what happened in life,
Gramma always had a Christmas tree. It
sat in front of the living room window, so

cheerfully decorated. I never tired of looking at the tinsel and the colorful, fancy ornaments. On this morning, hoping against hope I searched around the base of the tree. No presents of any kind, no doll. I knew better than to say anything and took my seat at the table.

After saying grace, Teddy said, "What's that in the corner?" Everyone mumbled that they didn't know. So he asked me directly and pointed to the corner of the dining room. "Where did that come from?"

I looked at the corner that he pointed to.

And there she was. The most beautiful doll I had ever seen. I actually gasped and covered my mouth with my hands. She had blond hair with pink ribbons in it, a lacy dress with a pink sash on her waist, white anklets, and little white shiny shoes - and her blue eyes looking at me. I had never in my short life felt such joy. I ran to her and hugged her. I danced around the room with her. I giggled. I wanted to cry.

Everyone at the table grinned from ear to ear. I do believe Gramma had the biggest smile of them all and even wiped away a tear. Grampa was clapping. Daddy picked me and my doll up, and we danced around the room while everyone sang Jingle Bells. It was wonderful. It was joyous. Everything was suddenly brighter.

I named her Mary Ann after my mother.

So yes, there is a Santa Claus. I never found out who mine was. But in my mind, it's the name for that family who knew how to make a sad little girl smile again.

DORIS AND THE KIDS

December 1, 1958, one of the most tragic fires in the nation's history took the lives of ninety-two children and three nuns at Our Lady of Angels Catholic elementary school on Chicago's West side.

My mother wasn't an affectionate mother, as mom's go. Few hugs and kisses came from her. But that was not unusual in that old, gritty neighborhood on the South side of Chicago. Being born and raised blocks from the stockyards during the Depression had its effects. It maimed one down to the very soul. Immigrant tenement housing, extreme poverty, and all that came with it either made you tough or destroyed you. You saw it in the eyes of many of the women around you. Mommy was no exception. She was a survivor. This made her, well, "contained" is the only word I can think of to describe her. Contained. There was often a hardness in her eyes and a restraint in her emotions, as if letting go and feeling things would make her a weaker person.

The day was December 1st, 1958. I just turned eight. When I walked out of school that day, Mommy and Grandma were standing on the corner. Since I lived only a block away, I was able to walk to school unescorted. Mommy hadn't met me outside of the school since the beginning of the first grade. So I knew something was not right.

Grandma was wringing her handkerchief. Mommy, well, she just had a strange look on her face as she came toward me.

"Where were you? You're late. What happened?" she asked, almost frantically. "I had to stay today and help Sister Kathleen clean our room. Remember? I told you."

"Oh God - that's right."

And then she hugged me. I was so shocked I couldn't even hug her back. Grandma cried silently in the background, muttering something in Lithuanian that I couldn't understand.

"What's a-matter?" I asked, still in my mother's bear hug. By this point I was getting scared. "What's wrong?"

"Did the nuns tell you anything?" She replied as she held my face in her hands.

"Bout what?"

"A fire."

"No, what fire? Where?" I looked in the direction of my house, feeling really panicky now.

"Dammit." She let out a long sigh as she stood back up.

"A school, on the west side, just like this one" she looked at the old wooden building that was our school. "It's on fire. Kids are getting burnt to death. It's horrible. It's all over the news. A Catholic school. They're jumping outta windows, for crissake" Mommy didn't sugar coat.

I looked at Grandma, who was now smiling as she wiped her tears. "I'm okay. Nothing happened here." I felt I had to reassure them both. Mommy looked down at me and smiled.

"I know. We just had to make sure"

I was feeling confused as she took my hand, another out of the ordinary act, and the three of us headed towards our house.

"Where's Pete?" I asked, referring to my older brother. "At home."

I had nothing else to say.

We lived in a two-flat that my grandparents owned. Gramps died a few years earlier. Grandma became our landlord out of necessity. It turns out she was right all along. Daddy was a bum. He was also sitting in prison.

Daddy wasn't a bad guy. He just couldn't keep a job. It turns out that the Friday paychecks that he was bringing home weren't from the box factory he said employed him. It was from a series of armed robberies. He hadn't worked at the factory for months, but was able to bring home a decent amount of cash.

They were small time heists, usually gas stations or currency exchanges around the city; a gun, a mask, late at night.

Heck, he made a decent living. Mommy never suspected a thing. He left for work every day. We never found out what he did all day while faking legitimate employment. He got caught because he got stupid.

He forgot that this one particular gas station was owned by our neighbor, Floyd. Even with a scarf across his mouth and a hat on, Floyd recognized this small-time hood with a gun. Now, Floyd was a big, surly, displaced Texan with a bad temper. When Daddy realized who he was holding a gun on, he ran. Floyd ran faster, tackled and "beat the snot out" of Daddy, as he put it. Then he called the cops.

It turns out that one of Daddy's other robberies was a bank. He had some help on that one. When the cops showed his mug shot to the bank employees, it turned his small time heist into a federal crime, and he was now sitting in the state penitentiary.

Mommy made sure we wrote to him every week. I drew pictures. Not too much an eight-year-old can write about. Pete did as he was told, but I could see the anger in his eyes as he wrote his letters.

Turns out, when you have a father that goes to the state pen, the other kids either stay away from you or make cruel jokes. The sins of the father fall on the shoulders of the children. To make matters worse, Floyd's daughter, Gerry, was my best friend in the whole world. That ended with the robbery. I never was sure why, but I cried a lot over it.

Grandma had to ask her paying tenants to move, and we replaced them. Mommy took a job as a waitress at a small restaurant a few blocks away. She worked the breakfast and lunch shift - 6:00 a.m. to 2:00 p.m., and Grandma got me and Pete off to school each morning. Mommy trudged home, exhausted, each day with her measly tips, then cooked and cleaned for us and tried to make ends meet. This made us inches away from dire poverty - as opposed to regular poverty, our current state. No toys for us. It was all about food, clothes, and a roof over our head. We knew better then to complain. Pete got a paper route and was promoted to man of the house.

Even though Daddy got us into this mess, I missed him. I know Mommy did. He was always full of jokes and laughter, almost like a kid. He made Mommy laugh. She hardly ever laughed now.

So that's where we were on that horrid, dismal, cold Chicago day.

Because of Daddy's short-term lucrative situation, we had one of the best televisions in the neighborhood. As a result, when we got to our house, several of the older neighborhood women (we called them bushas) were in our living room watching the tragic news. Grandma let them in when word spread of the fire. Many of the locals didn't own a television, and it wasn't unusual for them to come to our flat with Grandma to watch TV. Most days it was *I Love Lucy* or wrestling, but today it was pure tragedy unfolding.

Several of them squeezed my arm when I walked in. Aside from their hankies, a couple of them were clutching their rosaries and praying out loud.

The Our Lady of Angels neighborhood was the mirror image of our neighborhood, very ethnic; Lithuanian, Polish, Italian, many recent immigrants, Nuns as teachers, and Priests as neighborhood leaders and disciplinarians. It was just that it was on the West side of the city. These women sitting in our living room would have easily blended into that neighborhood. *I* would have had no problem blending into that neighborhood or that school.

I tried. I really tried to watch the news. The grainy black and white newsmen were obviously shaken up. Their words were awful. So I found myself doing "nananananna" in my head to drown them out and went into my bedroom.

Pete and I shared a room. He was lying on his twin bed reading a Batman comic book when I came in. Batman was his favorite. I was more partial to Superman and Supergirl.

"Hiya."

"Hi."

"Do you know about the fire?" I asked.

"Yeah, stupid, I know about the fire. Who doesn't?"

"Watcha doing?"

"Whatya think I'm doing? I'm reading." He was not in a good mood.

"You don't have to yell at me! Gosh."

He let out a loud groan.

"Just change your clothes and leave me alone. Don't be such a brat."

I couldn't figure out why he was being mean. He was usually a lot nicer. So I changed my clothes. I didn't want to leave the room, so I just sat on my bed.

"I'm going over to Dave's." he said abruptly. Dave was his best friend who lived next door. He stuck by Pete through all that had happened with our father.

After he left, I still wasn't about to leave the room, so I fished under my bed and got out the shoebox that held my paper dolls. Real dolls being out of the question, I had a decent collection of paper dolls that Mommy or Grandma would occasionally get for me. I kept the dolls and their rather large wardrobe in great condition in a shoebox.

I took out Doris. She was my favorite, a cute, cheeky blond, probably modeled after Doris Day. She was wearing a yellow bathing suit. I decided not to dress her with anything else that day. She had work to do. She was becoming

Super Doris. I overturned the shoe box that held the paper clothes. Flipped on its side, the box was much larger than Doris. I sent Doris on her first mission.

"Go save them, Doris," I ordered, and off she went.

Flying through the air, she looked down and saw the smoke. She landed at the side of the school/shoebox and immediately went into action. Her hands were bigger than the windows, so she was able to form a cup with her hands. The kids jumped in, and she placed them out of harm's way. She had one hand at each of the two windows, and a lot of kids in each hand.

Doris saw the firemen hard at work and moved even faster to get the kids out. She was even able to blow the smoke and flames away from the kids. Before I knew it, the building was empty, and the firemen had the blaze out. Everyone was saved, even the nuns. Everyone was cheering and calling Doris's name. I was cheering and calling Doris's name when my mother opened the door.

"What the heck are you in here yelling about?" She was obviously annoyed. I froze with Doris in midair.

"Nothing," I replied lamely, still holding Doris in midair.

"Nothing! The busha ladies can't even hear the TV. Put that stuff away. It's time for dinner. Where's your brother?"

"At Dave's"

"Clean up in here then go sit down. The soup will get cold. I'll get your brother"

"Okay" I said. I stared down at the scattered paper clothes and at Doris and began to clean up. But I kept Doris out.

"Good job, Doris." I said softly.
By the time I cleaned up and got to the table, Pete was there and eating.

Mommy never ate with us. She either busied herself or usually stood and watched us eat. I don't know when she actually ate. While we were eating, the Busha ladies left, and Grandma came in the kitchen, wringing her worn handkerchief. She started to tell us about the kids and what she had just watched when I cut her off.

"But Doris saved them" I said very loudly, out of the clear blue sky. As soon as I said it, I wanted to take it back. Even I realized that it was a strange thing to say.

"Huh?" said Pete.

"What?" said Mommy.

My grandmother looked at my mother and said something in Lithuanian.

"Nothing Ma. She's talking about something else." She said to her mother, then to me, "Eat your soup and be quiet."

I ate my soup and was quiet. I could hear the three of them talking around me, talking about children jumping out of windows and little bundles being taken out by firemen and priests saying the last rites. I tried real hard to think of Doris saving the kids as I ate my soup.

In the fifties when you went to Catholic school, it was mandatory that you go to mass before the school day started. There wasn't any missing mass. The nuns sat right behind you and did a head count. That morning, there were an unusually large number of adults. Before the mass the priest announced that this mass was being said for the children and the nuns that died in the fire. I looked around and saw both the men and women wiping away tears as they said their rosaries. I saw some of my classmates with clenched hands praying so intently that they were moving their lips. I found it hard to pray and just watched everyone else.

When we got to class, Sister Kathleen had us say one more prayer. Then she told us that the children and the nuns were with Jesus in heaven. They were special, and Jesus took them. They were happy and at peace with Jesus. They would be his new angels.

This certainly got me thinking. Since I had to pay attention during class, I did my thinking as I slowly walked home after school.

First of all, Jesus didn't seem like a friendly kind of guy. All I knew from holy cards and statues was a very severe adult who was in a lot of pain and suffered for us. He couldn't possibly be very pleasant and playful with all these new kids. He would be happy to have the nuns there though. I wondered if he would let the kids even fly with their new wings. After some thought, I was convinced that being with Jesus and the nuns would not be fun. I had visions of him saying there would be no flying. Instead they would have to drive around in a school bus, a bus in the clouds, which Jesus drove. The nuns would be praying from their prayer books and making the kids pray too, with an occasional break for a holy song. And Jesus would be making sure the kids behaved themselves. After all, he could not be in a very good mood, what with the crown of thorns and all that. I ran home as fast as I could to Doris.

Mommy was ironing and didn't pay too much attention to me as I bolted through the door and ran into my room. I got Doris out of her box and gave her instructions. "Doris." I said, "those kids ain't gonna be happy with Jesus and the nuns and a bus in the clouds. They need something fun. How about the beach? Where the water is cool and the sun is warm. Don't you think that would be better?" Doris nodded yes. So I kept her in her yellow bathing suit, and off to the bathroom we went.

We had an old claw-foot bathtub, which turned into the perfect, sunny beach. The slanted end would serve as the dunes that I remembered from our trips to the Indiana Dunes. I knew the kids would love running down the dunes and into the water. I turned the faucet on and created the lake.

"Okay, Doris, get the kids." I commanded. Before I knew it, she was surrounded by all the kids, who looked around at the beach and the dunes and the sun and at Doris. They sure looked happy. I could tell they were enjoying this. Doris began to sing a happy song about putting on a happy face. The kids soon followed her, singing as they marched along the beach and into the water.

And then it happened. Once Doris got wet, she literally fell apart in my hands.

The thin cardboard didn't hold up too well.

I began to shout. I began to cry.

"No. Doris, No! No! No! Don't go away Doris, the kids need you. Don't go away! Doris! NO!"

The next thing I knew, Mommy was shaking me.

"Snap out of it. What's going on? Look at me, Annie, look at me!!"

I looked at her, and all the grief, confusion, and fear came tumbling out. I was crying so hard I could hardly breathe.

I started stammering something about the kids who burned up, and Jesus and Doris. Finally, in between gasps of breath, I cried, "I don't want to burn up, Mommy. I don't want to burn up, too. I don't want to die, too." and I fell into her arms sobbing.

"Oh my poor baby, I won't let you burn up. You are not going to die on my watch. That's for sure."

I still was sobbing and shaking as she held me tight.

"I'm such a lousy mother. I'm not taking good enough care of you. God help me."

"Okay," she said as she pulled me away and started to dry my tears and wipe my nose with toilet paper.

"Ya know what we are going to do tonight?"

"W-what?" I stammered, trying to catch my breath.

"Well, first of all, no news on the TV. We are going to watch *I Love Lucy* or whatever you want. No Grandma and no busha ladies. They have to find another TV to watch, okay?"

I nodded yes.

"But before we do that, we are going to put on the record player and some jitterbug records, and I'm going to show you how to dance. It's about time for that. Okay?" I nodded again, sniffling. That sounded good.

"And before that, well, I brought home some donuts from the restaurant.

Would you like a donut?"

Things were looking up.

"Is there a chocolate one?" I asked, wiping at my still messy nose.

"Yes, there is a chocolate one."

"Okay." I mumbled.

"Good. What do you want to drink?'

"Coffee"

And my Mommy smiled and ran her fingers through my hair. "One chocolate donut and a cup of Joe, Toots." she said in her best waitress voice, then added, "Comin' right up!"

I was able to sigh and gave a little smile.

"Now wash your face. I'll clean up here later. And let's get this show on the road. Okay?"

"Okay," I said.

After she walked out, I just stood there staring at the door of this tiny bathroom. And I smiled.

My Mommy knew. She just knew. She made my world right again.

A MOTHER'S DAY

1968

The scream cut through the gentle spring morning like a blackened saber. Marlene sat up in her bed the moment the sound reached her ears. It came from the small cottage next door, Michael's house. Marlene's mother heard it too and had to stop her daughter from running outside without a robe or slippers.

"Oh God." she murmured, "don't let it be Michael. Please don't let it be Michael."

"Holy Mary, Mother of God, please don't let it be Michael." she prayed as she ran down the stairs. The shrieks became screams, then wails. She knew the sounds were coming from Michael's mother.

"Dear God in Heaven, help me, don't let it be Michael." She chanted. "Dear merciful God in Heaven, don't let it be Michael." She said loudly as she ran toward the house. She slowed when she saw the two military men standing by the doorway of Michael's house.

"All the saints in Heaven, help me." she moaned as she ran towards the front door, pushing the two men aside.

Michael's mother was on the floor, being held and caressed by her weeping husband. When he looked up at Marlene, nothing else needed to be said.

Marlene fled to the backyard, not knowing what to say or do, arms outstretched. Not Michael, no, not Michael. She began to vomit. She was aware that she was vomiting on the spring daffodils that had just come up. Her mother was suddenly there holding back her hair. The vomiting finally stopped, but the moans did not. The moans were now coming from her.

Sounds and voices stirred around her head in a grey swirling pool.

He died suddenly. It was a sniper in the jungle. They were on a routine patrol. He didn't suffer.

"It must be a mistake." she heard herself say to someone. "It can't be him. It's not possible."

Then she was in her bedroom. Faces surrounded her, someone was holding her as she wept. Her prayers stopped. Her body trembled.

There was always Michael. As long as she could remember there was always Michael. The families lived next door to each other for years, Michael's family in the small bungalow with the big front yard. His parents bought the house several years after arriving in America from war-torn Poland. Marlene's parents owned the two-flat next door and lived in the second floor. They were second generation Lithuanian. Marlene's father owned a hardware store nearby that once belonged to his father. It was a small store but one that always did very well.

Michael was a second child, born eight years after his sister, his only sibling. He was born almost two years before Marlene.

The two mothers got along well enough and often exchanged babysitting duties. They had little in common besides the children. If there was a social structure in this neighborhood, Marlene's mother was at the top. She was tall and thin, attractive, fashionably dressed, the wife of a business owner – Michael's mother, at the bottom of the social ladder, was short and heavier built and wore babushkas, loose fitting dresses, had a thick Polish accent and was the wife of a factory worker. She appeared older than she was. But on pleasant, warm days, they could be seen walking their children down the street towards the park - Michael toddling, Marlene in the stroller. Even at that very young age, Michael was fascinated by Marlene. If she dropped her toy, Michael picked it up for her. If she cried, he tried to calm her.

Marlene was an only child and had attached herself to Michael before she even realized she was doing so. As they got older, she followed him around the neighborhood, even when he was with his buddies. Some of his friends thought she was his baby sister. He didn't mind. It was Marlene. There was always Marlene.

Things changed when they became teenagers. Marlene went to an all-girl Catholic high school, and Michael went to an all-boy Catholic high school. After a long winter, one where they hardly saw each other, the two families got together after Easter mass. When Marlene walked into the room, nothing was ever the same again. She was a lovely young woman of sixteen. He was a handsome, young man in his senior year of high school.

Suddenly, they both saw each other in a different way.

To the delight of both families, Michael and Marlene began seeing each other as much as their schedules allowed. They both had part-time jobs and busy school schedules, but that didn't keep them apart. They were in love.

Architecture was the world that Michael wanted to inhabit. Even as a child he was fascinated by the structure and beauty of buildings. At the little neighborhood library, he read every book on Chicago history and architecture that they had. He took Marlene to downtown Chicago on most of their dates just to show her the historic buildings that surrounded them. Dinner and a movie was merely an afterthought. The structural details of the Board of Trade Building or the Tribune Building was what excited him. If they went to a baseball game, he would tell Marlene the history of Comiskey Park and hardly know a single player on the field.

With Marlene it was about becoming a nurse or, possibly in the distant future, a doctor. Medicine fascinated her in the same way that architecture fascinated Michael. She was on the road for a scholarship and had dreams of getting into the nursing program at the University of Chicago. She was on the Honor Roll and was elected the President of her Junior class and now the Senior class. Marlene was pretty, smart, and a source of pride not only to her parents but to the nuns and priests at the parish church.

In their soft, intimate moments, they spoke in raspy whispers of a wedding, of careers, of their dreams. They clung to each other. They laughed together. They shared their innermost thoughts. They knew what love was.

Then came Vietnam.

Michael had chosen to work for a year, so he could save money for college. That decision made him eligible for the draft. He had hoped he would be in college sooner, but that was not to be. There was just not enough money saved.

Then draft notice came. There was no choice. No one spoke of a choice. No one spoke very much anymore. His mother wept. When they did speak, his father brought up patriotic duty and how good this country had been to them.

Marlene's mother spoke of World War Two and lectured Marlene on how to handle being the girl left behind. Marlene kept her thoughts to herself. She wasn't feeling very patriotic. She just didn't want to make it any harder for Michael.

Marlene, in the middle of her senior year, knew all of her plans had been altered. The prom was no longer in the picture. It was graduation, working full time in the summer, and then college. Her new goal was to be ready for the day Michael came home from the service so that they could resume their life together. Now more then ever, she wanted to be married to him but knew that her parents would never allow it because she was still too young. But in her heart and in Michael's heart, they were married.

Nothing seemed to matter now, as Marlene lay in her bed clutching a stuffed lion that Michael had given her on her last birthday, her tears spent.

Somehow she made it through the next few days. Her mother let her stay at home that Monday but made her go back to school on Tuesday.

"You have final exams coming up and graduation after that. Do I have to remind you that as Senior Class President you have a speech to prepare? And we have to start shopping for a dress. There is a lot to do in the coming weeks." her mother coolly reminded her. It all sounded so irrelevant to Marlene.

"I know this is hard" her mother continued, "but you have a whole life ahead of you. Don't let this ruin everything."

Marlene could only stare back with unfocused eyes. So she went through the motions, accepting the condolences of her classmates, the nuns, the priests. She went back to her part-time job at the department store and managed to get through the hours. Life was lived in a bubble. It was when she got home, in the shelter of her room, that she wept the tears of her crushing grief.

The funeral mass was the following Saturday. There was no casket. Michael had not been brought home yet. It seemed an impossible feat for Marlene to get through. She didn't know how she could face his parents. She hadn't seen them since that awful morning. There was no room in her heart for sympathy, not yet.

The day was devoured by the sentiments, the condolences. Yes, they seemed to all repeat, she was young.

Yes, she would get through this. She would find another. Marlene didn't have the strength to argue.

Then there was the incense, the mass, the prayers, the knowing that she would never see these things in the same way again. Afterwards, she slept. It may have been the pills her mother insisted that she take, or it may have been that her young body and mind had to shut down for a while. But Marlene slept until late Sunday morning when she was awaken by the nausea that seemed to never leave her.

She bolted past her mother, who was getting ready for the Sunday mass, to the bathroom, where she wretched again and again, finally staggering into the kitchen and falling into a chair.

"Where's Dad?" She asked her mother.

"At nine o'clock mass he's an usher today." Her mother softly replied.

"Can I please have a glass of water?" She looked up to see her mother, frozen in place, staring at her.

"You've thrown up a lot these last few days." Her mother replied.

"Yeah, what do you expect? Ever since we got the news I can't seem to stop." She said, holding her head in her hands.

Instead of getting her water, her mother began pacing around the little kitchen.

"When did you have your last - you know."

"My last what? What do you mean?" Marlene frowned, not in the mood for this.

"You know what I mean - your last god damn period! You know damn well what I mean!"

Marlene jumped. Her mother never raised her voice at her, much less curse at her.

"I don't know." She stammered. "With, with all this going on, I don't know."

"Well think, damn it. Think!" her mother's voice getting even louder and more urgent.

"I am. I am! Maybe before, I think, maybe before when Michael was home on leave or..."

Marlene got no further when her mother slapped her in the face, a slap so hard that it lifted her off of her chair. She lay on the kitchen floor, too shocked to comprehend what had happened. She realized that when she was hit she saw stars, for a second, just like in the cartoons.

In her entire short life, her mother never struck her, not once. Now she was standing over her daughter, speaking in a voice that Marlene could barely recognize.

"You slut! How could you?!" her mother screeched. "You open your legs to the first boy who wants it, and now you're knocked up! How could you? You stupid tramp!"

The words continued. "What are they going to say? The nuns, the priests?" The screeching became mixed with tears. "How could you be so stupid? We didn't raise a slut in this house, but we got one - a slut, a tramp! I can't believe this is happening."

Marlene could only stare back in confusion.

"Get out of my sight!" her mother yelled. "Get in your room. Who do you think is going to raise this baby? Huh? Well it ain't gonna be us! Get out of my sight! I have to figure out what the hell we're going to do with you and your bastard."

Marlene crawled on her hands and knees to her bedroom, knowing she didn't dare try to stand, afraid of another slap, still reeling from the first one.

Her mother did not leave for mass. Instead Marlene could still hear her pacing, sobbing and cursing, becoming another person that Marlene didn't know existed. The words blasted through her brain – slut, tramp...knocked up, baby, bastard.

Lying in her bed, Marlene picked at the rose on the floral wallpaper. Her mother had chosen it the year before, but Marlene always hated it and now more than ever. When her father came home she put a pillow over her head to drown out the words and thought back to another day, a day she revisited often.

***

"This is not how I wanted it to be." Michael said. "I wanted the Palmer House or the Hilton. Not this."

They looked around the dismal motel room with the worn furniture and stale odor.

"It shouldn't be like this for our first time. Hell, they think we're downtown watching a movie or something. It's just not right."

"Michael," Marlene said, trying to hide her nervousness. "It doesn't matter. I don't care. We'll go to the Palmer House for our honeymoon. It's not important. Really. I just want to be with you."

"I know. You're right. It's just not what I wanted for us. We not doing something dirty or wrong."

She took his hand.

"So now what?" she asked. "As you know, I've never done this before."

"That makes two of us" Michael said with a small grin. "Number One. Take your clothes off."

Marlene started to giggle and blush. "I can't just take my clothes off!"

"Well, I do know that you can't do it with your clothes on." He replied, laughing.

"Damn nuns." Marlene said. "They really screw you up with all that talk about saving yourself and sin, and so on, and so on. Now I can't bring myself to do anything."

"Hey, from what I understand, and from what I've read, it comes naturally. And believe me I've read a lot."

Both of them began laughing.

"Hey, it's me." He said. "It's just me, Michael. The love of your life."

"You are so right about that."
Marlene responded sincerely.

Michael took her in his arms and
gently kissed her.

And it did come naturally. As the
passion became more intense, the
awkwardness disappeared. Marlene felt
the sharp pain, but felt the gentleness
afterwards. They touched each other like
they never had before. They felt the
hunger. They felt the beat of their hearts.
They felt the love that they had for each
other. By the end of the afternoon, they
rested quietly in each other's arms, spent
but happy.

"Not bad for the first time." Michael
said.

"I think we did it more than once. I
lost count." Marlene grinned. "What
time is it?"

"Almost four." Michael replied.

"Do we really have to leave soon?
I've grown to love this smelly old room."

"Yeah, Ma invited everyone she
could think of for this big farewell
party. Christ, I'm only going to basic
training."

"Only?" Marlene said, sitting up.
"Only going to basic training. Its eight
weeks. God, Michael, how am I going to

do this? Eight weeks. I can't stand the thought of it."

"Oh please Mar, don't start crying. That's more than I could take."

"I'm not crying. I'm just saying this is going to be so hard. I'll miss you so much. I love you so much."

"I know, Babe. I know. I'll miss you too, and I love you too. But you'll see me in eight weeks, looking bald; muscular and bald. Say good-bye to this great head of hair." Michael said, trying to sound casual but dreading all that was ahead of him.

Marlene left the bed, grabbed her clothes and went to the bathroom. She couldn't continue talking, not with the knowledge that Vietnam was likely once basic training was over. The word Vietnam was never spoken between them. She hoped and prayed that he would be sent to Germany. That happened sometimes. It happened to her friend's brother. They sent him to Germany instead of Vietnam. She prayed for Germany.

When they got home, they sat silently in the car staring ahead.

"I'm not going to your house." Marlene said. "I can't draw this out any more."

"I understand."

"What time do you have to leave?"

"Five o'clock in the morning. Christ, it'll still be dark out." "I'll be up."

"You don't have to, you know."

"I'll be up." Marlene insisted. "Look up at my back porch. I'll be there. Wave at me.

"You sure?"

"Of course." She knew she had to lighten the mood.

"I can't bear a long drawn out good bye. So I'm going home now. See? No tears. Don't forget to write. See ya soon." She gave him a peck on the cheek and quickly left the car, fighting the tears that she knew he didn't want to see.

Michael grinned. He understood. He, too, was fighting back the tears.

Marlene spent that night in a chair wrapped in a blanket on the enclosed back porch. She knew sleep wouldn't come. Not after what she had experienced that afternoon.

At five o'clock that morning she saw Michael and his father as they left the house.

Michael turned in the direction of her porch. She had a small light on so she knew that he saw her. He waved. She waved back.

Eight weeks later, Michael was home - in uniform and with very short hair. His buddies and family joked with him, trying to make light of the changes in him. He tried to laugh back. But it was a forced laughter. Marlene wanted to laugh and tease him as well, the way she did before the army came into their lives. But she couldn't make it happen. The news had been delivered. Michael was going to Vietnam.

His last leave was a short one and their time together cut even shorter by Marlene's job and school. There seemed to be an endless trickle of friends and family that wanted time with Michael. He couldn't say no, even though he just wanted to be with Marlene.

Once again, on his last day home, they went to the same motel, the same room.

This time there was very little talking. With a passion that seemed boundless they clawed at each other, trying to diminish the pain that they both felt.

Afterwards, in the motel parking lot, Marlene looked over at Michael. He was motionless, staring ahead.

"Michael, what is it?"

"I can't Mar. I just can't."

"Can't what?

"I'm not a killer. I can't go to some fucking god-forsaken jungle and kill people."

Marlene saw that his hands shook.

"It's not me. I'm not like those guys in basic who talked about killing gooks. I don't want to do this. I want to marry you. I want to go to school and become an architect. I want a family. I want a future."

With that he broke down in tears, clutching the steering wheel until Marlene reached over and took him in her arms.

She had never seen him cry, even as a child. So she held him, caressed him, unsure of what to say, until his tears were spent. She knew he was right. He wasn't a killer. He was a good and gentle man, an architect. This was all wrong. A horrible mistake, a bad dream that included the both of them. There were no words that could make it right.

Once again – a scene repeated.

"What time do you leave in the morning?" she asked. "Six" he replied softly.

"I'll be on the back porch again." "Okay"

This time there was no short peck on the cheek. She reached for him.

86

"I will love you, every minute of every day for the rest of my life. Come back to me my love. Please come back to me." she pleaded.

"I'll do whatever I have to just so I can get back to you. I love you so much. But if I don't..."

She cut him off. "Don't say that. Please don't even think that."

"I will always be with you Marlene. Always."

"I know. And I will always, always be with you."

With that she broke away and went home. Her parents spoke to her, but she didn't know what they were saying. She took her blanket, sat in the chair by the porch window and began the vigil.

It was lighter now. Once again she saw Michael and his father leave the house.

This time she could see Michael's mother, clutching what looked like a dish towel, wiping her tears as her son walked away. He stopped to look up at the porch window and waved. She waved back and he was gone. Only then did she let herself cry.

* * *

"You shouldn't pick at the wallpaper. It'll make your mother mad." Marlene jumped at the sound of her father's voice. It was such a ridiculous comment, she almost laughed.

"I think she's already a little mad about something." She appreciated her father's calm tone.

He sat at the end of the bed while Marlene continued to pick at the wallpaper. "Here's what we're gonna do" he began, prefacing this comment with a long sigh.

"Come end of July, beginning of August, you'll go to Michigan to live with your Aunt Agnes until the time comes. We'll tell everyone that you're going to college out there, and you have to be a Michigan resident to get lower tuition, so you decided to go live with Agnes."

He let out another sigh.

"We'll work it out with Agnes. You know she's nuts about you, and you'll be a big help to her now that Lee passed away. She needs the company out there in the middle of nowhere and with no kids to help her out. You could drive her around, since she doesn't drive, and do things for her. Heck, she's my sister, and I helped her out a lot, with money, you know, over the years. She owes me a good turn.

And like I said, she likes you so much, I'm sure she'll keep your secret." He paused to clear his throat. "Then when the time comes, you hand the kid over to the adoption agency, and it's over. The kid gets a good life, and you go on with yours. No one needs to know.

Marlene remained silent and motionless.

"We all make mistakes, but you fix 'em and go on with your life. There'll be other guys and eventually you find someone, get married, and have all the kids you can handle. Maybe even become a nurse, like you want."

She heard someone down the street was cutting grass. How normal, she thought. How incredibly normal.

"Okay, so that's what we'll do. Your mother will calm down. Just don't say nothin' to your friends, or no one. You understand? That kind a news would spread like a wildfire."

Marlene remained silent.

"So just do what we say and it'll all work out. Someday, you'll thank us." He left the room.

A week later, Marlene stood at the front door to Michael's house. Before she had a chance to knock, Michael's mother opened the door. Standing before her was a gaunt old woman that bore little resemblance to the mother of Michael that she knew through the years.

"Marlene" Sophia said softly. Marlene always loved her accent and the way she pronounced her name.

"Hello, Sophia. Can I come in?"

"Yes, Yes, come in." she replied "Sit, sit, you want tea?"

"No, no, I came to talk to you. Is Henry home?"

"No, he go to church. I..." she stammered. "I no go no more. I-- I mad at God."

"Me too. I'm very mad at God." Marlene said with an understanding smile. "Sit by me. I need to tell you something."

Sophia quietly sat next to her on the small sofa. "What? Tell me."

"You've known me all my life Sophia. You know I'm a good person." Sophia nodded.

"You know that I loved Michael with all my heart."

Another nod as she took Marlene's hand.

"I'm not a tramp. And Michael was the only boy ever in my life."

"Yes, I know. You good girl."

"We wanted to get married."

Sophia gave a small smile.

Marlene gave up a long sigh and wiped the hair from her face. She was sweating. "I'm pregnant with Michael's baby."

The look of shock on Sophia's face was one that Marlene would never forget. She let go of Marlene's hand, silently stood up and went to the front window, her back to Marlene.

"My parents," Marlene continued quickly. "My parents want to send me to live with my aunt in Michigan and give the baby up for adoption."

"Sophia, I will not do that. Instead, I will spend the money that I have saved for college to get a small flat. I already spoke to my boss, and I'll start working full-time next week. They don't know about my condition, and I won't tell them until I have to. Hopefully, I won't get fired."

She couldn't look at Sophia anymore and spoke to the wall.

"I will not, under any circumstances, give up this baby. I turn eighteen next month, and my parents can no longer make decisions for me. Hopefully, somehow down the road, I'll be able to go to college. I still want to be a nurse. Sophia, I will have Michael's baby."

91

Sophia finally spoke. "Michael's baby. Michael's baby. You having Michael's baby. Oh my god!"

Standing before Marlene was a transformed woman. Sophia was laughing and crying at the same time. She pulled Marlene to her and hugged her. Repeating "Michael's baby" over and over again.

Soon Marlene was laughing and crying as well. Tears of joy fell from both their cheeks. "I help you. I know people with flats where you can live. I watch baby, Michael's baby when you go work. I help you. Not your mama. You no give baby away. Michael's father, he help too. We both help. We have Michael's baby. Yes. Yes! We have Michael's baby. And I go to Church. I not mad at God no more."

1983 - Washington D.C.
Vietnam Veteran's Memorial

Marlene watched as her son looked for his father's name among so many on the black reflective wall. She didn't move when he told her that he had found it.

Michael's parents stood in the distance, looking overwhelmed, looking afraid, holding on to each other.

She slowly walked over to him. Seeing Michael's name jolted her more then she expected. It was so long ago but felt so recent. It was a struggle to hold back the tears.

"Mom?"

"Yes?" She looked down at the teenage boy who so resembled his father. The eyes, the cut of his chin, the hair.

"I know you told me a lot of stuff about him, but like, could you tell me again? Like all kinds of stuff."

"Of course I will, hon." She smiled.

"He'd be proud of you, Mom, being a nurse and all, and raising me."

"Yes, I think he would. And he would be so very proud of you too, Paul." Marlene said as she softly touched the letters of Michael's name.

There will always be Michael, she
thought. The love doesn't die.

PRIVATE WORLDS

This was reality. And it being realty, I knew it was not going to be good.

Fantasies and daydreams were my preferred reaction to life. I tended to drift off into my daydreams while humming the Rolling Stones song, "Gimme Shelter".

It wasn't going to work now. She was dying, and there wasn't a damn thing anyone could do about it. *Face it*, I said to myself. *Just deal with it.*

But how do you deal with this sick, emaciated woman in this hospital bed who was my mother? I now knew her secret. I found out so late in life. That was the part that seemed to bother me the most.

In walked Father Joe, parish priest to many. But, it turns out, father Joe to me; the secret of the ages. The secret finally passed on to me through her drug induced state a few days ago, fifty years after the fact.

She was a married woman. He was then and is now, a much respected parish priest, expected to be celibate. An affair; A scandal. He was sent away to Florida. She followed him, with her husband. Apparently, the man that I thought of as my father kept up the charade until the day that he died 18 years ago. Father Joe now an aging pastor of our Catholic parish.

I never knew. I feel such rage, such confusion. I should be feeling overwhelming grief at my mother's deathbed. But I am angry. I was born of deceit.

He sees my face – the anger and the grief. I see my blue eyes looking back at me. He knows that I know. Words are useless. He tries to say something, but remains mute. He looks down at the shadow of the woman that he loved but never truly had.

He chose the church over her. She lived in his shadow, grasping at moments. He christened me. Did he know then? At my graduation, at my wedding. He was such a close friend of the family, for a parish priest. He christened my children, his grandchildren. So many questions.

Tears are falling from him now. He kisses her hand and mutters endearments. I leave the room. For her sake I give them privacy.

Can she hear him? In spite of my feelings, I want her to know that he is with her. Does she know he's there? I want it to be so.

Was he worth it? Was it all worth it? I want to ask.

I'm overwhelmed. I'm defeated by the lies. My emotions can't keep up.

I had fallen back into my private world of daydreams again.

OPENING DAY

1975

It comes to me in my dreams now, but I know it's more than a dream. It's a memory, a fragile, cherished memory. It's opening day for the White Sox at Comiskey Park. I walk through the turnstile with my Uncle Ed. We purchase our programs, bypass the food vendor because, of course, we only ate our hot dogs and drank our beer during the game. But we take in the smell of beer and those hot dogs, and head for our seats. But it's that sensation, after you've walked through the tunnel and stand at the top of the stairs. It's right there. And it never failed to thrill me. It's the sight of that radiant green field with the white bases and the pitcher's mound. It always stopped me in my tracks and brought a smile to my face. It was baseball season. It was spring, and once again I was at opening day with my uncle. I knew what the man meant when he said "Déjà vu all over again."

The tradition began when I was nine, when Uncle Ed saw me trading my baseball cards with the other kids on the block. It was apparent that I knew more about the players and the game then they did, and I was a girl. I don't remember when I developed this passion for baseball, but I do remember following the games on the radio. When the games began to be shown on the little black and white television, I was mesmerized. That was when Uncle Ed promised, and it was a promise that he never broke, that we would go to every opening day home game. It was Uncle Ed who called the school to say I was sick. Once I entered the work force, it was Uncle Ed who called my employers to say I was sick. It was Uncle Ed who brought the blanket if the Chicago April weather felt like February.

Truth be told, I'm sure he would have rather been there with his younger brother, my dad, but World War II put an end to that. Daddy died in the war, but Uncle Ed filled in as a dad the best he could.

If Uncle Ed had a passion, it was for baseball, the White Sox and Comiskey Park. He went to his first game when he was eight. He always boasted that he snuck into the park to see this game, which he probably had to, since money for a baseball game would have been hard to come by. But from that first game on, he did whatever he had to do to see a game. As he got older and had better paying jobs, he went to as many games as he could and saw the greatest players of their day.

It became our little ritual. He would regale me with the names, the scores, and the outcomes of some of the most memorable games he had seen. And he could usually tell me where he sat during these games.

"That was where we were sitting when the Babe almost hit one out of the park." He would say as he pointed to the left field upper deck. "Heck, almost out of the city. I swore that ball was going to end up in Wisconsin. Much as I hated him, boy, that man could hit."

Yes, he saw them all. The names flew off his tongue like he was referring to his old friends. I guess in a way they were his friends – Shoeless Joe Jackson, Lou Gehrig, Ted Williams, Mickey Mantle, Joe DiMaggio, Jackie Robinson, and others. Unfortunately, most of the great players were usually on the opposing teams and usually part of the hated

101

Yankees. But then came Minnie Minoso and the 1959 pennant – but no World Series Championship. He even went north to Wrigley Field to see Stan Musial play. And no true White Sox fan ever went to Wrigley Field. He never told anyone but me that he had committed such a daring act. Uncle Ed just loved great baseball.

Usually, I loved hearing the stories, even if I had heard them dozens of times before. But today was different. I was distracted. I kept glancing at the two empty seats that Uncle Ed purchased tickets for. He caught me looking.

"Don't worry. She'll show up." He said, trying to reassure me.

I wasn't so sure. The seat was for Mom, Mommy, Mother, Mama, Patricia. Whatever affectation she chose for the event. She was coming straight from O'Hare Airport by cab, after her flight from Miami. Originally, it was going to be for her and her husband. He backed out at the last minute. Actually, he ran out at the last minute. He saw that she got on the plane, then called me.

"She's on the plane. She's all yours." He blabbered when he called me. "I can't do it anymore. I'm done with her. Don't bother sending her back." Then he hung up. This was husband number three. But the number of men in her life had far exceeded that number. It was the same story. They fell in love with her at first, the beautiful, sexy, party girl who loved to drink and was quick to jump in the sack. They always thought they got lucky. They didn't.

The madness usually manifested itself early in the relationship. It took many forms; unfounded jealousy, out-of-control anger, hysterical, manic laughter, and the mood swings. I saw it all. I knew all the signs. These men didn't. The tics, the frightening change that came through her eyes, the twitches of her lips. I had a lifetime of learning all about Patricia and her demons. Most of the time, I could soothe her, control her. I learned how to when I was very young, probably about four or five. I had been taking care of her for a long time. When I failed, she was off to an institution, and I was off to a relative's home.

Mother couldn't hold down a job, so we usually lived with her parents. But when they shipped her off, they shipped me off too. I guess they needed a break from both of us. I always just wished that they would send me with her, so we could be together.

So my childhood was a series of different homes and different relatives, depending on the situation with my mother. The only constant was Uncle Ed. He was always there, keeping an eye on things. He would have taken me in, but he and his wife, Aunt Sophie, were childless. And Sophie was determined to keep it that way. She was also afraid of my mother and afraid of what I may have inherited.

What no one understood was that I loved her. She was my mother. She never hurt me. Quite the opposite - she was my playmate. We played with my dolls. We went to the park and she swung on the swings with me. Unlike the other mothers who sat on the benches and watched their children play she joined in, giggling and playing with all of us kids. That qualified her as nuts to the other mothers.

She was all I truly had in the world, except for Uncle Ed.

The Sox took the field. I always loved that part, too. I always cheered loud and clapped hard. The seasons usually ended in disappointment, but you didn't know that on opening day. They might just do it this year. There may just be a superstar in that group on the field. It just remained to be seen.

By the 4th inning, I couldn't keep my mind on the game. My stomach was churning and I was on the brink of panic. Where could she be? The flight landed hours ago. What did she tell the cab driver? What strange location did she ask to be driven to?

"They used to say she was nervous. She had bad nerves," my uncle suddenly blurted out.

"What?" I replied.

"That's what they called it when she was young. They said she was just nervous. Your dad, though, well, he was just head over heels in love with her. He could calm her down. He never saw what other people saw. He just loved her, and she just loved him." This was unexpected. My uncle never spoke much about my parents or the war or his childhood. Some things, it seemed to me, were simply out of bounds when we spoke.

So I wanted him to continue. I just looked at him and hoped he would. Besides the game was going nowhere.

"Did you know they met when she was just out of the eighth grade?" he asked. "I don't know much. No one seems to want to talk about them, never did."

"Yeah, some things are like that." He continued. "Anyway, they started hanging around with a group of kids, the way kids do at that age. And that was it. They were together all the time. Now, she was too young to be going out with boys, and he was two years older than her, but, boy oh boy, they saw something in each other, and there was no keeping them apart. They started out as buddies, but that changed soon enough"

We stopped talking long enough to clap at a good play by the right fielder.

"By the time she was getting ready to graduate from high school, all they talked about was getting hitched. My parents didn't seem too happy about it, and I think her parents were just happy to get her outta the house. She was already acting nervous, like I said. I think they were afraid she would get knocked up and not be married. So a couple of days after graduation they were married. And sure enough she was knocked up."

I had to stop him. The math wasn't making sense.

Before I could, he interjected, "Bet you didn't know about that either." he said as he shook his head. "Baby boy. He only lived a couple of hours."

I felt my jaw drop. I once had a brother.

"Yeah, well, if she was just nervous before, this made her screwy. But somehow, and it wasn't easy, my kid brother could handle her."

We were both quiet while we pretended to watch the game. I needed another beer and so did he. He called the beer man over.

"Go on." I said as we drank our beers.

"Well, then came that goddamn war. I had my bad foot and couldn't go, but your dad went. He was one of those that enlisted after Pearl Harbor. Before you know it, he's all suited up, looking real handsome, and she's back at her folk's house. She didn't take it too well that he enlisted. I remember her bawling a lot. When he came home on leave before going overseas, well, that's when she got pregnant with you."

I found myself wishing we weren't at this game.

"Then what?" I said. "Tell me, please. I know he died on D-Day. That's all I know."

I also knew that my uncle never really got over it. He was my dad's best friend as well as his brother. He looked up at the scoreboard and shook his head. I was afraid he wouldn't continue. Thankfully, he did.

"We get that goddamn telegram delivered to us. The army didn't have Patty's folks' address, just ours. Well, my folks and me, we were pretty broken up, but someone had to tell Patty. So they sent me." He paused. "You never heard such screaming. She kept on hitting me. The neighbors talked about it for a long time. They had to get the doctor over to give her something."

"Poor Patty, that's what really made her crazy. She wasn't strong enough to handle what life dishes out. Never got over it. Her parents had to take care of you a lot. That's when they started sending her to those blasted hospitals. She kept saying that he was in the room with her, and she was always talking to him like he was there. Shit like that. You know the rest."

"Yeah, I know the rest." I could picture this poor heartbroken woman, my mother, racked with grief and confusion. I could see it like I was there.

"We had a lot of good times though. Your dad, Patty and me. We came to a lot of these games and spent a hellava lot of time at the bars around here. Your dad probably loved baseball more than I do. He wanted to play. But who goes out for baseball, especially then? You went to work as soon as you were old enough to bring in a couple of bucks, even if it was at a hell-hole slaughter house. That's where my folks ended up after they got here from Poland. Did you know that?"

I nodded yes.

"Your old man and me sold newspapers and swept floors in taverns. Ya did what you had to." He paused and smiled. "But we made sure we had fun, and we sure as hell made sure we came here to see the Sox. We always found the cash for that."

"I'm worried. Where is she? It's already the seventh inning."

"She'll get here. She knows this park as well as I do. She knows where we'll be sitting."

Suddenly, I heard her. I stood up and looked at the top of the steps, and there she was. "Abby, Abby, Where are you?" Her hands were cupped around her mouth and she was frantically screaming as loud as she could.

She got the usher's attention, too. There were two of them next to her. What a sight she was. She was wearing a long flowing kaftan in shades of bright orange and brown and yellow.

And she had dyed her hair. I suppose it was meant to be red, but came out orange - bright, flaming orange. She looked like a butterfly, a beautiful monarch butterfly.

I ran as quickly as I could up the stairs and into her arms. I was always the happiest in her arms.

"Oh Abby, oh Abby, I almost went to Wrigley Field. The driver couldn't understand me. I know I said Comiskey Park. Why would he take me there? I would never go there. I'm a White Sox fan."

"It doesn't matter, mom. As long as you're here. I missed you so much!" I could feel the tears of relief."

I could also see my uncle behind me. "Hello, Patty. Long time no see." He smiled.

"Hi, Ed" she said softly. She almost looked embarrassed.

"Doesn't she look great, Uncle?" I know I was beaming at her. "She looks like a monarch butterfly."

"A what?" my mom said, wide eyed.

"A monarch butterfly, in your browns and orange and yellows. You look like a monarch butterfly."

"I guess I do. What with these big long sleeves and my red hair. Do you like my hair? I dyed it myself."

"I love it, Mom."

"Oh no. Not 'Mom'. I'm Patrice. It's so much more modern. So Ed, and you too, Abigail, you must call me Patrice."

"Patty, really?" my uncle moaned.

"Patrice, simply Patrice."

"Jesus Christ. Ok, Patrice," he said, drawing it out.

"It's still beautiful, isn't it?" she said looking around at the worn old ballpark where she, and now I, had so many memories.

"Yes Patrice, it's still beautiful," my uncle said.

"Some good times, right, Ed?"

"Right, Patrice." He gave her a small understanding smile and nodded. "Let's get out of here," Uncle Ed said. "It's a lousy game and I could use a real drink."

"Can we go to McCuddy's?" she asked, referring to the bar across from the ballpark that also held so many memories.

"Sure Patrice," I said. "Let's go to McCuddy's and have a round."

"Such good times," she repeated. "And now that I'm a monarch butterfly maybe I can fly there."

We all three laughed as we slowly walked toward the 35th Street exit. I caught Uncle Ed looking up and around as we were leaving. I also caught him as he wiped a tear from his eye.

Uncle Ed passed away that October, after the World Series, with the sports page in one hand and a Camel cigarette in the other. If he could have chosen a way to go that would have been it.

I never went to another White Sox game again.

Patrice came to live with me. But she took my comment too literally. That following spring, wearing her kaftan, she decided to fly off the roof of my four story apartment building. Someone heard her call my father's name before she jumped. Some people are not meant to live life. It's just too difficult, too confusing. I was able to let her go. I understood.

I moved to Arizona. I never married. Since I had no one to answer to, Phoenix became the place to grieve and start a new life. I never went back to Chicago. The south side and Comiskey Park were consigned to my memories, to be revisited only mentally from time to time. But when I read that the park was being demolished, I wept. I wept for all that was.

But you can't demolish memories. So as the wrecking ball burst through the solid old white walls, I imagined every speck of dust carrying one of the memories that were created at that park. And the memories floated out and over the City of Chicago, to places where they live forever.

Anton's Story

Anton swore so loud that the people on the streetcar could hear him as it drove away.

While getting off the streetcar he stepped into a large, dirty pool of water. There was a hole in his shoe, and despite the layer of cardboard he used to fill it in, the filthy water seeped in, soaking his foot with every step. The cuss words didn't begin to convey the misery that he was feeling on this brutally hot August day.

Anton wanted a drink. He had the shakes. He needed a drink very badly. He had no money and knew he would have to settle for the rotgut that he kept hidden in his attic.

It was a gray day; the kind of day where one couldn't tell if it was morning or afternoon. But Anton knew what time it was. He knew by the pains in his bones that he felt after a long day at the stockyards - a day of hauling carcasses and slashing carcasses and smelling the blood of carcasses. With the pains, he carried the lingering smells that even a steaming bath at the bath house on the corner could not wash away.

Slowly he walked home. Home to a wife who barely looked at him and when she did he could see the hatred in her eyes. Home to his children who, except for the youngest, were no longer gentle little children. They were older now and were either indifferent to him or fearful of him.

Anton knew he deserved this. He drank and when he drank, he beat his wife, his children, and anyone who got in his way. There was a devil inside of him – a raging, rabid devil. A fiend struggling to get out and let everyone know what a failure Anton was. A failure as a provider, as a husband, as a father, and as a decent human being.

How did this happen? Anton wondered. Where had he parted ways with the man that he once was - only to become this creature? He remembered stories from his childhood in Lithuania- stories of monstrous green- eyed dragons that destroyed everything in their path with its fiery breath. In Anton's mind, this is what he had become.

It was the Russians. It always came back to the Russians and the cobbler. The cobbler who came through his village every few weeks looking for shoes to repair for a small pittance or a meal. It was the cobbler who brought news he picked up as he went from village to village lugging his bag of tools.

Anton and his family had just sat down to a meal when he arrived, so he was invited to join them and share what news and gossip he had. In the course of the conversation he looked at Anton, who was the oldest of the four children sitting at the table.

"How old are you?" He asked.

"Why do you need to know that?" Anton's father said, never giving Anton a chance to answer.

"The Russians," the cobbler said.

"What about them?" Anton's father despised the Russians, who had taken over his country. The stories of their brutality were well known.

"He'll be old enough to join their army," the cobbler responded, looking at Anton.

Anton's mother froze. Her spoon clattered when it hit the floor. "No," she muttered. "He's only 16. He's a boy."

"Do you think they care? He can shoot a gun, can't he?" the cobbler calmly replied. "They're taking them from the fields. These fiends need the cannon fodder. They're going to war again."

"War?" said Anton's father. "With who?"

"Some place far. It's called Japan. Wherever the hell that is."

"You know that for sure?"

"I hear a lot of things in my travels. Most of what I hear is true. So what I hear is this - they take them from the fields, from their homes and make them soldiers. You go. No choice. They call it conscription, another name for hell."

No one spoke. The cobbler continued.

"In the village Dabrupine, they made everyone gather in the square. One of the officers tapped the men on the chest with his riding crop. He told them they had a half hour to get their things and say good-bye. No choice. They were surrounded by soldiers with rifles."

He shook his head at the memory of the weeping women who related the incident. "There was a lot of wailing that night. The wives, mothers, and children."

The army. Anton's blood ran cold. He always thought he would be a farmer like his father. They were not wealthy but had enough to get by on. Their cottage was a good one – one big room, but solid and sturdy with a big fireplace. His mother's spinning wheel sat in the corner, where she spun the threads that eventually became their clothing. He and his siblings slept in the loft overlooking the big room. His family lived in the area for as long as anyone remembered. He could not imagine living anywhere else or doing anything else. The thought of war and killing was beyond his imagination.

"He's not going nowhere." his father stated "He has to work the farm with me. He stays here."

The cobbler wiped his mouth with the back of his hand and stared at Anton's father.

"Like I said – you have nothing to say about it. They just take them."

Silence filled the air. Everyone stopped eating. "It can't be true." said his mother softly.

"It's true. You should send him to America, away from all this shit. That's where all the young people are going. When I go to these villages, there's always someone leaving for America. You have a chance there – away from the Russian dogs, maybe make some money, make something of yourself. If I were a young man, I would go."

He paused and looked at Anton.

"Go to America. Better than getting shot in some pisshole and not having any life at all."

"Thank you for the meal." With that the cobbler left the table, grabbed his hat, and walked out of the cottage

Throughout the night, Anton could hear his parents muffled argument. He heard his mother weep. He heard his father curse.

The next morning Anton's father was not in the barn tending to the cows. "Where's Papa?" he asked his mother, as she silently kneaded the bread dough. "He went to town."

"What for? He never goes to town in the middle of the week." Anton asked, knowing the answer.

"He has to find out how much money we need for the ticket," she responded never taking her eyes off the dough. "The ticket for the boat."

"No. Mama, no, I don't want to go. No. Mama." Panic seized him. He stomped around the room shaking his head. "No, I belong here. I can't go."

"Be quiet" she said, her voice trembling. "It's decided. You cannot stay here. I will not have my son in the Russian army. You go. Make a new life.

You're young. You will go. You will go with the others."

Anton couldn't bring himself to speak or to move. "Go milk the cows. They can't wait all day. Go." He could only stare at her.

"Go!" she screamed, "Go milk the cows! There is nothing else to say." He saw the tears in her eyes.

Two weeks later he had the money, a letter of reference, and other paperwork that he was told was so very important. One of the young cows and two chickens were gone, so he knew where the money came from. Guilt tugged at him when he realized what his family had to sacrifice to send him to America.

Soon people from his village, as well as some of the other villages, came to the cottage to give him names of their relatives that lived in America and to tell him stories that they had heard. He tried very hard not to show how afraid he was.

On the morning of the day that he was leaving, he saw the cobbler off in the distance, standing beneath a tree. He gave Anton a tip of his hat, smiled, and walked towards the road. Anton cursed him as he walked slowly into the cottage.

"I will come back someday, Mama." he said to his mother. She was sitting in her rocker, in front of the fireplace that held only burning embers. She stared ahead, clutching the arms of the rocker, as if gripping this chair could stop the inevitable.

"No, no, you won't. You will make money. Get married, have children. You won't come back."

"Yes, I will. I promise."

"Do not make promises that you cannot keep. You are a man now, and you must do what a man must do." She slowly rose from her chair.

"Send us letters. It is good that you know how to read and write. The priest will read them to us. Tell us your stories about America. But most important - don't forget us. Tell your friends and then your wife and children and one day, your grandchildren - tell them about us. Tell them about where you came from."

"I will, Mama" Anton replied, fighting back the tears. "I will."

"Be a good man, Anton, be a good man." She hugged him tightly and turned back quickly to the fireplace.

Be a good man, Anton. Be a good man. The words echoed in his head after all these years. She lived long enough to see his wedding picture, but not long enough to see the pictures of her grandchildren. He was glad she knew nothing of the wretched journey in steerage, of the fear and confusion of Ellis Island, or of the way his soul was ripped from him while working in the Pennsylvania mines.

But he did try to be a good man. He took the young, pretty woman that he married and his new daughter to Chicago, thinking it couldn't be worse than the mines. He worked in a slaughterhouse not making enough for his growing family. They lived in a cramped apartment, surrounded by taverns and men like him.

Men who drank to forget, men looking for some laughter, trying to find some escape from the gloom that engulfed them. Men, so overpowered by all that surrounded them that many of them no longer felt like men.

Weariness overtook him as he stood in front of the four-flat he called home. Opening the door, he was hit with the usual odor of old damp wood and of countless meals that seeped through the closed apartment doors.

He quietly, slowly entered the kitchen. At first his family didn't even notice that he was standing there.

His wife spoke first. "Wash up. Food is almost ready. You smell bad."

His teenage son said nothing, but Anton could feel the fear coming from him. How could a son be so fearful of his father? But Anton knew. It came from years of drunken tirades and undeserved beatings.

The older daughter said nothing and continued to help her mother with the meal. She never spoke to him unless she had to. The V shaped scar on her arm, from being pushed into a glass door by her drunken father was a constant reminder of why she hated him so.

But then there was his youngest, his little Stella, always his favorite. Was it because her difficult birth almost killed her and her mother on that hot, July day twelve years prior, or was it because she looked so much like his younger sister whom he left behind all those years ago in Lithuania? Whatever the reason, she made him feel gentle again. She made him less brutal.

The family sensed this and at times used her to calm him down when he was in a drunken rage. He could never hit her as he did his wife and other children. No matter how severe one of his drunken rages could be, she was the only one who was able to say or do something to stop the madness. More than once, she had thrown herself at him when he blindly began slapping his wife. Her plaintive cries were enough to make him stop. She would take him by the hand and lead him to his bed, where he would sprawl out, mumbling apologies. She would stay at his side until he finally slept.

"Hi Papa." She smiled at him. It was her smile that made him feel so undeserving.

"Hello, my little one," he said softly, as he gently stroked her blond hair. He then walked out of the room to the stairs that led to the attic. He suddenly felt a strong melancholy that he had never felt before, a melancholy that replaced his feelings of anger and desperation.

Once there, he began to rummage through all the places where he hid his bottles. The bottles were gone. His wife had found them. This he knew since it had happened before.

Anton stood, sweating in the stifling heat of the enclosed attic, no longer wanting a drink.

He saw the rope. The rope that his wife used to hang the wet laundry on in the winter months. "It's not a bottle that I need anymore." He said to the empty space around him.

He reached for the rope and pressed it against his face. A sense of resignation was setting in. The solution was so easy, so quick, he thought.

"There is only one way to kill the monster. There was only one way to end this misery." He was staggering, as if drunk and spoke loudly once again to the vacant space. "They will all be better off without me."

The thoughts hammered at his brain, shutting off any reason.

"I can't do this anymore. I can't be the drunk anymore who beats his family. I can't be a monster anymore. So tired of being poor, of struggling, year after year, day after day. So tired of being a failure. So tired of reaching for the bottle." He leaned against a post and looked above at the attic beam.

"No more. It must end. It must end." He continually muttered. Somewhere inside of him, he felt that if he stopped speaking to this vacant space, he would lose what little courage he had left. He shoved aside any lingering thoughts that tried to intrude.

"Anton, do this. It has to end." He repeated now with determination. He wiped away his tears, and took a deep breath.

A chair was nearby. He placed it under a beam. Swiftly, deliberately he began to tie the knot. He stepped on the chair and tossed the rope over the beam.

"Papa, what are you doing?"

He jerked at the sound. He looked down to see his young daughter Stella staring back at him.

"Papa, the food is ready. Ma said to get you. What are you doing with the rope?" She looked at it in his hands. She fought the image it was creating.

Anton felt strangely embarrassed. He stepped down quickly and sat in the chair. "Nothing, little one. Nothing"

"Papa, oh no, Papa." She sounded terrified when the realization set in. Anton could see it in her eyes. He wanted to make a joke but was at a loss for words. What could he possibly say? The rope dropped to the floor. He feebly tried to kick it away. He forced himself to smile at her.

"You can't Papa. You can't ever. You can't leave me. No Papa." Anton could see panic building inside of her.

"No, Papa, Please no!" she pleaded.

"It's fine. This is good. You come to me, and I'm alright. See?" he said, his words tumbling out, his body suddenly shaking. "I won't leave you. I am fine.

Don't worry about your Papa. Don't worry. I won't leave my little girl."

He meant it. Something he could not define was suddenly lifted from his damaged soul.

Something that was a part of this little girl, something that made him want to live again.

Without another word, his daughter ran to him and hugged him. Her tears mingled with his as they held each other.

"Never do that again Papa. Promise me, Papa. Never again, please." She finally said wiping her tears.

"No little one, never again. I promise. I promise."

"You're a good man Papa. You are a very good man."

"I am not."

"Yes, yes, you are my Papa. A good man. Inside you are a very good man."

Anton looked down at the floor, unable to respond.

"Let's go downstairs and eat. I won't tell no one. I promise. Please Papa. Ma's waiting."

"Come with me."

Anton nodded and took her hand, silently vowing to somehow become the father that she deserved.

"Yes, my little one, let's go and eat our dinner. Your Papa is hungry."

The Travelers

When you look to the past you
see us. When you shuffle
through old wooden boxes,
dresser drawers and broken
suitcases you see us.

We are sepia-toned, brides and
grooms, hardly touching. We are
children posing before a static
background on the day of their First
Communion. We are old ladies in
babushkas and old men in suits that
were hardly ever worn.

We were so much more than that.

We came from farms and villages,
many of us fleeing the constant wars
that ravaged our homelands, others
looking for a way out of the grinding
poverty that ate at our souls. We
saw horizons without hope.

We were looking for something better, something that would offer freedom, peace, and a chance for a better life.

We left knowing that we were leaving behind our parents, our brothers and sisters, our friends, our way of life. We left knowing that we would never return.

So we left, some of us so very young, by horse cart to the trains, then to bustling, deafening ports. The sight of the enormous ship left us staring ...awestruck.

Any excitement that we may have felt at the point was quashed by living with the sights and fetid smells of traveling in steerage.

And the fear, there was so much fear mixed with our tears.

But then there was the lady with the torch and an island named Ellis. And more fear, more chaos, and more towering buildings. There were more trains and more strangers speaking in languages that we didn't understand. We held on to each other.

When we reached our destinations – more huge structures and cramped housing and foul smells. We stood in wonderment.

Is this what we came for? Were we fools? No, we would show them that we were not fools.

We worked in the coal mines of Pennsylvania. We slaughtered pigs and cows and stood in their entrails in the stockyards of Chicago.

Our children were taken out of school to work, although the nuns and priests protested. We saved our money and our dignity.

Then we bought our own houses, started our own businesses, and went to our churches. Our children began to thrive. We held our heads up high.

Our children worked hard. Many fought for this country and died for this country. Their children graduated from high schools and colleges. They also fought and died for this country.

We survived. We prevailed.

So, yes, look to us for answers and inspiration. That is as it should be, for you are here because we were there.

We are part of your creation.

Tell our stories.

Visit our graves.

Say our names.

Don't let us be forgotten.

NOTE: Page 136 is the last page in the book.